The
Ouija Board

The Ouija Board

A Doorway to the Occult

Edmond C. Gruss

PUBLISHING
P.O. BOX 817 • PHILLIPSBURG • NEW JERSEY 08865

Library of Congress Cataloging-in-Publication Data

Gruss, Edmond C.
    The Ouija board : a doorway to the occult / Edmond C. Gruss.
        p.   cm.
    Includes bibliographical references and index.
    ISBN 0-87552-247-5
    1. Ouija board. 2. Occultism—Controversial literature. 3. Oc-
cultism—Religious aspects—Christianity. I. Title.
BF1343.G77   1994
133.9'3—dc20   94–13493

Contents

Preface

Why another book on an occult-related subject, particularly one with specific and extensive attention to the Ouija board? After thirty years of teaching courses on history, religious cults, and the occult, I have seen fresh challenges to Christianity and the biblical worldview arise again and again, requiring renewed attention. These assaults do not go away by ignoring them. My earlier studies on the Ouija board (*What About the Ouija Board?* [1973], *The Ouija Board: Doorway to the Occult* [1975], and *The Ouija Board* [1986]) are no longer in print. Yet new books, articles, films, and other media sources continue to appear that encourage psychic and occult experimentation. Because new generations of adults and young people still buy and use Ouija boards, we need clear warning, explanation, and interpretation from a Christian perspective.

My interest in the subject goes back a number of years. My class on religions of America includes a section on spiritualism, and students frequently wanted to discuss the Ouija board. Many times students shared their own experiences or that of others they knew. Periodically, parents, pastors, or youth workers contacted me for information about the Ouija board because their own children, church youth, or even adults were experimenting with it. In my attempts to answer these requests, I found little material written from a Christian or even non-Christian viewpoint. Secular sources often encourage people to experience psychic development through the Ouija board. In 1992 I requested information on the Ouija board from over a hundred ministries, individuals, or organizations that specialize in the occult. I discovered no new publications dealing specifically with the Ouija board.

Many years ago, as a freshman in high school, my son presented a talk on the occult. His teacher was surprised that I would not allow him to play with the Ouija board—after all, he said, "It's just a game." This attitude is still prevalent among Christian parents and church leaders—some have even used Ouija boards themselves or have given them as gifts. Through my research, I have learned about some of the adverse effects experienced by users of the board. These range from dramatic manifestations, such as demonic obsession or possession, to radical perversions of belief systems. One is reminded of 1 Timothy 4:1: "The Spirit clearly says that in later times some will abandon the faith, and follow deceiving spirits and things taught by demons" (NIV). Many who have been deceived by the Ouija board are certain that they have been "enlightened."

My study has convinced me that the Ouija board is one of the most popular but least understood *occult* devices in our culture. Although some books on the occult may mention the Ouija board on their dust jackets or covers, the reader searches in vain for any significant treatment of this topic within the book itself.

My purposes in writing this book are to provide factual information on the Ouija board, to warn of its possible dangers, to demonstrate its importance as an occult tool, and to provide a biblical and historical perspective and interpretation.

Because of the nature of the subject, I have needed to use sources that are at odds with my Christian perspective—some are spiritualists, others reject both spiritualism and the supernatural, and some advocate experimentation with the psychic and occult. The factual information these sources provide can be valuable; for example, their observation and discussion of specific cases. But their interpretation of these phenomena may be starkly at variance with my own interpretation, which is based on a Christian worldview. The reader should understand that my quotation or use of such material is not an endorsement of a non-Christian worldview. Because this study is necessarily limited, I encourage the reader to consult the material in the notes and those publications which are suggested for further reading.

This book is the result of years of contact with college students, Christian friends, and the many who have shared their experiences in various ways. Special thanks go to my friend and colleague John Hotchkiss, who worked with me on an earlier version of this book and who also reviewed the present study, and to Claire Hughes, who encouraged me and did so much to strengthen this effort through her suggestions and skillful editing. I wish to thank my wife of forty years who has typed every manuscript for every article and book I have written.

Finally, I would like to thank the staff at Presbyterian and Reformed Publishing Company for their interest and encouragement and for their part in carrying this book through to completion.

Introduction

In 1985 I happened to notice an announcement in my local paper about "The Ouija Project," which was to have two showings in the Modular Theater at the local Institute of the Arts ("In the Neighborhood," *Daily News* [Woodland Hills, CA], January 22, 1985). I learned little about the performance from the telephone number provided, but the student who was producing the "Project" promised to leave information for me at the theater. When I picked up his reply to my questions, I noticed a number of posters displaying the familiar names of the Parker Brothers' product. "Ouija" and "Mystifying Oracle" are registered trademarks of Parker Brothers of the General Mills Fun Group. *Ouija board* often is used in a generic sense to refer to homemade devices that are used like the Parker Brothers' product. The student's note explained: "'The Ouija Project' is a theater installation. The board is 32 by 24 feet, and the marker is 8 by 6 1/2 feet. The audience is encouraged to enter the installation space and use the board." (It should be remembered that the commercial board is just 18 by 12 inches.) "The Ouija Project" intrigued me and I decided to go see it.

After arriving early at the theater, I listened to the conversation of the largely student audience of about two hundred as they waited for the theater to open. Some were explaining the various theories of what made devices like the Ouija board work. Others discussed their own experiences with the board or those they had heard about. As we entered, I could see on the stage below the gigantic board and message indicator, reproduced in minute detail and surrounded by props to create the atmosphere of a fortune teller's establishment. After a brief explanation of the rules, members of the audience were invited to come down from the elevated viewing area in groups of ten to fifteen at a time to work the board. After placing their finger tips on the table-height Ouija pointer, the participants and members of the audience began to direct questions to the board. At first the pointer remained stationary, but then it slowly began to move. Finally, with great speed and ease, it glided on its casters over the board. Sometimes the answers were spelled out so swiftly it was difficult for the participants to keep up with it.

The first questions were mundane or general: "Will I go to Europe?" "Will I go to Dallas?" "Will there be an earthquake this year?" And then the questions took a more serious turn: "Are there any spirits present?" "Are the spirits male or female?" "Is the spirit happy?" At one point, a participant asked the audience: "Do you have any dead relatives you want to talk to?" Other questions related to the future and to life on other planets. Still others dealt with religious issues such as, "Is there a God?" "Is there a devil?" and even, "Is Reagan the anti-Christ?" Although the answers the board gave were not always significant, the movement of the pointer was—it convinced the participants that they were not doing it themselves. They even got down on their knees to look under the pointer for a motor or other means of locomotion.

Later I interviewed the graduate student who directed the "Ouija Project." I learned that a number of people had asked him how he made the table move. When he first conceived the project, he believed it would be necessary to plant certain people among the participants to ensure that the pointer moved. But in the actual demonstration, he claimed that the pointer moved without such help. In fact, he was as surprised at its speed and ease of movement as the audience. The student also explained that a friend who had worked on a previous Ouija project with him did not wish to participate in this one. Several other friends that were involved in Ouija board use experienced subsequent problems. One group that participated in a Ouija board seance on campus reported some "serious contact" and were quite affected by the experience. Upon further questioning, the student admitted that he had little factual information about the board, its operation, and its history.

My encounter with "The Ouija Project" demonstrates that fascination with the Ouija board is still very much alive, though information and understanding of the board are limited. Whether the king-sized Ouija board actually worked is not the issue. What is significant is the public's interest in such a device, their belief that it could answer questions (whatever the source), and their conviction that the indicator actually moved without the conscious effort of the participants. Millions of people still use the conventional Ouija board, and many others will use it in the future. Ouija board users seriously believe that they communicate with dead people and with spirits. Even if the messages are spelled out as the result of subconscious muscular movement (as many believe), the board is hardly a game or harmless pastime.

This study will touch upon a number of commonly asked questions about the Ouija board:

- Who invented the Ouija board, and where did such devices originate?
- How does the board work? If the Ouija board "talks," where do the messages come from?
- Why do many people believe that the Ouija board can be used to make contact with the supernatural realm?
- If the Ouija board just reflects the subconscious thoughts of those using it, why could this be dangerous?

- Why do many experts warn against experimentation with the Ouija board?
- Since it is often sold in stores that sell toys, why should children not be allowed to play with the Ouija board?
- Is there any truth to stories about the Ouija board having been involved in cases of mental illness, possession, suicide, and murder?
- Is there a connection between the Ouija board and the involvement of young people in the occult or Satanism?
- Did the Ouija board play a part in starting the modern channeling movement?
- Can the use of the Ouija board actually lead to events such as those depicted in *The Exorcist?*
- Is there any connection between the Ouija board and what the Bible says about demons, demon activity, and possession?
- What is the biblical perspective on Ouija board messages?
- What should a person do if he or she is presently using a Ouija board?

1

The Ouija Board: A Doorway to the Occult

The following true accounts are significant but by no means unique. They serve merely as an introduction to a serious subject—the Ouija board as a doorway to the occult. The use of this so-called game is fraught with real danger.

Thirteen-year-old Robbie lived in a Maryland suburb with his father, mother, and grandmother. The following account of his life is taken from *Possessed: The True Story of an Exorcism* by Thomas B. Allen.[1] His life was fairly typical of others his age, with one exception—he preferred board games to sports. As an only child, Robbie often depended on other adults for entertainment, especially his aunt Harriet, who was his father's sister and a frequent visitor in his home. She "responded to Robbie's interest in board games by introducing him to a new one—the Ouija board." After having the board and its use explained to him, "Robbie was fascinated. He enjoyed the skittering movement of the planchette as it skimmed about, veering from one letter to the next, spelling out answers to questions that he or Aunt Harriet asked." Aunt Harriet was a spiritualist who was convinced that departed spirits could be contacted through the Ouija board. Because Robbie was accustomed to solitary amusements, he sometimes played the Ouija board by himself. Robbie's mother was not a spiritualist, but she did share a few of Aunt Harriet's beliefs. Aunt Harriet explained that spirits also could communicate by rapping on tables and walls, and by other physical methods.

Strange occurrences began to happen in Robbie's home on January 15, 1949. The boy and his grandmother were home alone when they heard a dripping sound. They checked the faucets but could not locate the source of the noise. Then an even stranger thing happened: they "saw a painting of Christ begin to shake, as if somebody were bumping the wall behind the painting." By the time Robbie's parents returned home, the dripping sound had ceased, but it was replaced by the sound of "scratching, as if claws were scraping across wood." This phenomenon continued for several nights.

Aunt Harriet died on January 26, 1949. Robbie was devastated by her death and turned to the Ouija board for solace, sometimes using it for hours at a time. Probably he was trying to use the Ouija board to contact Aunt Harriet. New manifestations began to occur: the sound of squeaking shoes followed by the sound of marching feet; a knocking sound in answer to a request for a verification of Aunt Harriet's presence. Finally the family heard a scratching sound from *inside* the boy's mattress that continued "night after night, for more than three weeks." The mattress shook violently and the bedcovers were pulled taut, as if they had been starched. Robbie's desk at school would move in a planchettelike fashion. At home, various articles and furniture moved, levitated, or flew.

Allen investigated the actual case depicted in the movie *The Exorcist*. He "researched every fact and tracked down every living witness to the exorcisms of the Mount Rainier boy"depicted in the movie.[2] Allen provides new information on the relation between the Ouija board and spiritualism and the terrifying events the boy and his family experienced. This case and Allen's book were featured twice on "Inside Edition."[3]

During her freshman year in college, Miss C. and three other girls began playing with a Ouija board when they grew bored with bridge. Their play quickly developed into an obsession when they started receiving amazing answers to questions—answers that were clearly beyond their knowledge. For example, one of the questions they asked the board was: "What was the gross national product of Brazil in 1966?" One of the girls wrote down the answer (which was given in millions of dollars), and then they all went to the college library to track down the information. To their amazement, the figure in the resource book exactly matched the one they had written down. Stunned by their success, they began asking similar questions. Soon they were working the board every evening. This sort of growing obsession is fairly typical of Ouija board users.

Several months later, the girls decided to ask for the name of their spirit contact, and the planchette spelled out the name "George." Then they asked George where he came from, and the word _hell_ was spelled out. Their curiosity next led them to inquire about the date when each of them would die. All but one of the dates ranged from forty to sixty years in the future; however, one girl's death date was within that year. This so terrified the girls that they stopped playing with the board. On the exact day that the board had predicted, the girl in question was killed as her car plunged through a guardrail on a California coast highway. The police had no explanation for the accident—the girl had not been depressed or suicidal, and weather and traffic conditions were normal. As a result of the tragic death of her friend, Miss C. became a Christian.[4]

Peter Anderson, an evangelist with Christian Ministries in Leicester, England, speaks on the occult in schools and churches. He recounts this experience.[5] A fifteen-year-old girl named Ann, an apparently normal, well-balanced teenager, was found dead in bed with a polythene bag over her head. She left a suicide note in which she stated: "If it is possible for a spirit to return, I shall return. If there are no signs of ghostly disturbance within a week of my death, then the spirit of the human body is beyond human recall." At Ann's inquest, the Lancashire coroner commented:

> It has come to my notice that there is an interest in spiritualism at this girl's school. I have been told that there has been involvement with a Ouija board, and girls are trying to contact the spirits. I hope that Ann's death will serve as a lesson to her school friends not to get involved in spiritualism—it is dangerous.[6]

Anderson also noted that the headmaster of another Lancashire school confided "that he was worried by the fact that the boys affected by the occult were not the emotionally unstable or unintelligent members of the school community. In some schools even members of the staff had instigated seances."[7] One of the boys in that school recounted this alarming Ouija board episode:

> "One evening when we were playing with the Ouija board . . . we asked the controlling spirit, 'When will the end of the world be?' The board was picked up by an unseen force and torn completely in halves and a cupboard in the corner was knocked over." No one slept that night![8]

Anderson records several other cases that appeared in the press or that were related to him by those involved.[9]

On February 12, 1993, the television show "Sightings" (Fox TV) featured the Ouija board. One brief account concerns the experience of an anonymous Ouija board user. She explains her terrifying encounter:

When I first started using the Ouija board it was just for fun. And then, about a year ago, I took it out and something happened, and I got scared, and I put it away. And I went to bed. It was about 1:00, 1:30, and I kept feeling like there was something or someone in the room. And, I tried to get up, and I was pushed down. This tremendous force on my chest was picking me up and throwing me back down again. I felt like I was being attacked. I grabbed the sheets and tried to hold down to the bed, but I couldn't. I felt like I was being raped.[10]

As illustrated in the following excerpts from a letter to Ed and Lorraine Warren, authors and experts on the topic of demonology, such sexual assaults are not unusual for those who use the Ouija board. After four years of using the Ouija board, a woman wrote:

My life is being dominated by this demon. Dear God, how can I tell you! Every day it viciously rapes, sodomizes and beats me. . . . Now I am virtually bedridden and in constant pain. It has not stopped torturing me since the first day. Violent beatings, stabbings, constant rape, that's all this demon does to me. . . . It does all it can to force me to commit suicide! Constant badgering and berating. Verbal abuse so foul and sickening and dirty it is unbelievable! I feel more than half dead. Please, please help me.[11]

*D*r. Hans Holzer, well-known author and parapsychologist, tells the story of forty-nine-year-old Mrs. G.,[12] who in the spring of 1964 was a financially secure woman with the leisure to do whatever she wanted. Her friend saw an advertisement in the local paper for a spiritualist church, and thinking that this sounded entertaining, Mrs. G. accompanied her friend to the meeting the following evening. Their first experience was fairly satisfying, so they returned a second time. They overheard two members of the church discussing the success one of them had in using a Ouija board.

Mrs. G. had viewed the Ouija board as merely a toy, but since she had little to occupy her time, it intrigued her, and she bought one. The first time she used it, she had instant success—it felt as if some outside force were energizing the planchette. Quite unexpectedly, the planchette spelled out the following statement: "Hello, this is John W." John W. was a former suitor of Mrs. G.'s whose affections she had spurned and with whom she had had no contact for thirty years. She put the board away but curiosity impelled her to take it out again. The planchette spelled out a torrent of words, expressing John W.'s love for her.

Mrs. G. became obsessed with the Ouija board and "for hours, she would listen to the alleged John W. tell her how much he wanted to stay with her, now that he had found her again." This obsession led to a personality change that her husband noticed. By the winter of 1964, "in addition to the frequent Ouija board sessions, she now began to hear the man's voice *directly.*" The voice repeatedly told her that it was with her and whether it came from inside or outside her head, she was never alone. "She threw away the accursed Ouija board that had opened the floodgates to the invasion from beyond. But it did not help much." John W.'s presence became more invasive—she felt his presence with her even when she was in bed. One night she felt as if her heart was being squeezed—like a heart attack. More than anything, she wanted to return to the life she had before using the Ouija board.

Finally Mrs. G. explained the full extent of her suffering to her husband. In her search for relief, she underwent physical and psychiatric examinations. She read books dealing with possession and tried automatic writing. She was even hypnotized, but nothing helped. In desperation she contemplated suicide. After a session with a hypnotist, she returned home in hopes that John W. would leave, "but the molesting continued unabated." Eventually she experienced release.

The subject of the Ouija board is a serious one. The experiences in this chapter span several decades and involve both male and female subjects from varying age groups. The results of these experiences include terror, suicide, unexplained accidental death, unusual presences, physical manifestations, and sexual attacks. But they all have one thing in common—involvement with the Ouija board—a device with ancient antecedents. In the next chapter, we will trace the board's ancestry and modern history.

Notes

1. Thomas B. Allen, _Possessed: The True Story of an Exorcism_ (New York: Doubleday, 1993), 2–9. Allen is a recognized author of sixteen books and a contributing editor to _National Geographic_. Malachi Martin, an expert on exorcisms, commends Allen for his investigative research.
2. Ibid., dust jacket.
3. May 10, 1993 and July 19, 1993.
4. Miss C. recounted these events in 1968 to friends in her Campus Crusade group at Vanderbilt University.
5. Peter Anderson, _Satan's Snare: The Influence of the Occult_ (Welwyn, England: Evangelical Press, 1988), 23.
6. Ibid.
7. Ibid.
8. Ibid.
9. Ibid., 21–24.
10. Penny Rich, another Ouija user featured on "Sightings" remarked: "The Ouija board is not a toy, and it is not a game, and I would like very much to see it taken out of toy stores."
11. Stoker Hunt, _Ouija: The Most Dangerous Game_ (New York: Barnes and Noble, 1985), 67–68.
12. The following account comes from Hans Holzer, _Ghosts, Hauntings and Possessions_ (St. Paul, Minn.: Llewellyn, 1991), 198–206.

2

The History of the Ouija Board

The occultism craze that swept America during the 1960s skyrocketed Ouija board sales, which in 1967 outsold Monopoly®. Evelyn M. Cuoco (Parker Brothers' Consumer Relations Administrator) notes that for a few years sales of the Ouija board "hovered around the 2 million mark" and that it continues to be "a very solid Parker [Brothers] staple" (letter to the author, May 5, 1992). These figures demonstrate a strong resurgence of interest in the Ouija board, even though few people know anything of its ancestry or the meaning of the word *Ouija*. Misinformation about the board abounds, as is evident in journalist John Godwin's poll of 1972 and in more recent surveys.

> I picked out a fairly random lot of thirty dedicated Ouija players and asked them if they could tell me where the game originated and what the name meant. Most of them, as it turned out, believed that it was a Far Eastern device, its origins lost in antiquity, its ti-

tle meaning something or other in either Chinese, Hindi or Korean. One lone individualist held out for Hebrew, another had it on the authority of her card-reading girlfriend that Ouija meant "spirit" in either Sanskrit or Persian.[1]

None of the players correctly identified the meaning of the word *Ouija* or the origin of the board game, which was patented in the United States in 1891. The name *Ouija* is simply a combination of the French *oui* and the German *ja*—both words meaning "yes." But the players were correct in assuming the antiquity of its ancestry—similar devices were known to the Egyptians and other ancient peoples.[2]

The Ancestry of the Ouija Board

Nandor Fodor, a psychical researcher, indicates that devices used like a Ouija board were

> in use in the days of Pythagoras, about 540 B.C. According to a French historical account of the philosopher's life, his sect held frequent seances or circles at which "a mystic table, moving on wheels, moved towards signs, which the philosopher and his pupil, Philolaus, interpreted to the audience as being revelations supposedly from the unseen world."[3]

Another writer describes a similar instrument as "a pointer that indicated various Greek letters carved on a slab of stone. A modern equivalent is called the Ouija board."[4]

Fourth-century Byzantine historian Ammianus Marcellinus records one of the earliest detailed accounts of divination, which used a pendulum and a dish engraved with the alphabet. He tells how Fidustius, Patricius, and Hilarius were arrested for divining the name of the emperor who would succeed Valens (A.D. 364–78). In his testimony before the court, Hilarius explained their procedure: one person held a ring suspended from a thread over the center of a round metal dish that had the letters of the alphabet engraved on the rim. When they operated the instrument, it spelled out the first letters of the name Theodosius (Theodorus).[5] In an effort to prevent this prognostication from being fulfilled, Valens had his great General Theodosius killed. But the prediction became reality despite his efforts, for after Valens' death, the Roman Emperor Gratian invited Theodosius' son (Theodosius) to become emperor in the East.

A less sophisticated method of divination that was also common in Roman times used a ring suspended by a thread in (or within reach of) a glass vessel. To obtain answers to questions, participants recited the letters of the alphabet. Whenever a correct letter was mentioned, the ring struck the glass. Another method was to ask questions that could be answered by "yes" (one strike) or by "no" (two strikes).[6]

The use of divination devices in ancient times was not restricted to the West. The Chinese used a form of the planchette before its invention in Europe. In the *North-China Herald*, Dr. Macgowan gave the following description of this type of spirit communication:

> The table is sprinkled equally with bran, flour, dust, or other powder; and two mediums sit down at opposite sides with their hands on the table. A hemispherical basket, eight inches in diameter, is now reversed, and laid down with its edges resting on the tips of one or two fingers of the two mediums. This basket is to act as penholder; and a reed, or style, is fastened to the rim, or a chopstick thrust through the interstices, with the point touching the powdered table.[7]

Chinese operators invoked the spirits and waited for a response. Basket-planchettes were also used in the West.[8]

In Africa, the Azande of the Congo used a device they called the rubbing board, actually a primitive Ouija. The rubbing board is a miniature table, carved out of wood, which has two straight legs and a sort of curved tail, together with another piece of wood the size of the table top, which is slid around on the latter by means of an upright handle. The juice or soft meat of a certain fruit is put on the table top, and the opposite part is moistened and put down over it, and pushed back and forth. Such is the quality of the juice and the two pieces of wood that the upper piece either goes on gliding smoothly over the lower, or else it soon sticks to it quite tightly, so that it cannot be pushed back and forth and has to be pulled off.

. . . the worker simply asks the board a question, telling it to stick for a yes and slide for a no. It usually acts definitely, either sliding smoothly or sticking promptly, and so it gives the impression that it knows what it is saying and has no doubt in its mind.[9]

Another form of divination that became popular during the Victorian era was called table-tipping, table-tilting, or more aptly, table-tapping. But the practice

is as old as occultism. Even in ancient Greece people knew about the strange behavior of certain three-legged stools or tables under conditions involving the strange powers of the psychic world. Like so much of the extrasensory ability in man, this too was condemned as witchcraft and black magic during the Middle Ages and after.[10]

The procedure for table-tipping involves a seancelike atmosphere and a prearranged set of signals for "yes," "no," "don't know," and "uncertain." Participants gather around a table with their fingertips lightly touching its surface. While the group concentrates, one or more members address questions to the table. People have claimed that tables sometimes have moved across the floor, tilted up, levitated (on rare occasions), or rapped out messages. A further refinement in table-tipping was the substitution of the recited alphabet for signals; table-tapping occurred when the appropriate letter was mentioned. Sometimes the table rapped out a predetermined alphabetic code (one rap = a, two raps = b, etc.). Some even have claimed that communication occasionally has taken place without any movement of the table at all, but by raps within the wood of the table itself.[11]

Table-tipping seemed an awkward and time-consuming method of spirit communication, so in 1853 a French spiritualist invented the "planchette." "Although not commercially mass-produced in the United States until the 1860s, planchettes imported from France were available in spiritualist bookstores by the late 1850s."[12] The planchette is described in detail in a book published during this period.

> The planchette is a little heart-shaped table with three legs, one of which is a pointed lead-pencil, that can be slipped in and out of a socket, and by means of which marks can be made on paper. The other two legs have casters attached, which can be easily moved in any direction. The size of this table is usually seven inches long and five wide. At the apex of the heart is the socket, lined with rubber, through which the pencil is thrust [see figure 1].[13]

Today the planchette's shape and size varies with the manufacturer, but the basic instrument remains the same. To operate it, one or more people lightly place their hands on the planchette, allowing it to move freely over the paper and without consciously attempting to aid it. When the participants are successful, the planchette writes words and sentences. Automatic writing is similar but does not use a planchette—the person merely holds a pencil loosely in his or her hand and allows the pencil to write "automatically."

THE BOSTON
PLANCHETTE
From the Original Pattern, first made in Boston in 1860.

Figure 1.

The Ouija board was born when the planchette's pencil was replaced with two additional legs (*modern* Ouijas have only three legs), and a board with an alphabet, numbers, and words was added.

The Invention of the Ouija Board

William Fuld of Baltimore is usually credited with the invention of the Ouija board. But if a patent establishes priority, Elijah Bond is the inventor since he first filed for a patent on May 28, 1890 (which was granted on February 10, 1891; see figure 2). Bond even called his invention the "Ouija or Egyptian luck-board." The first page of Elijah Bond's patent (No. 446,054) assigns it to Charles W. Kennard and William H. Maupin.[14] On December 30, 1890, the Kennard Novelty Company filed an application for the *Ouija* trademark, and it was registered on February 3, 1891 (No. 18,919). Fuld was granted a patent on July 19, 1892, for an improved version

13

(No Model.)

E. J. BOND.
TOY OR GAME.

No. 446,054.   Patented Feb. 10, 1891.

Fig. 1.

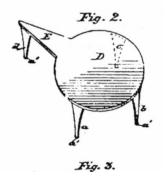

Fig. 2.

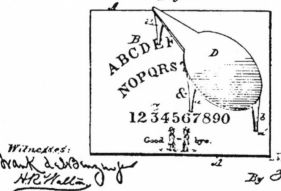

Fig. 3.

Witnesses:
Frank d. Benjwfr
H. R. Hall

Inventor:
Elijah J. Bond
By T. C. Brecht
Attorney.

Figure 2.

14

of the *pointer* (see figure 3).[15] According to Edgar Goodman:

> The Kennard Novelty Company did a big business.
> There was a split in the firm. Kennard broke with the
> partners he had taken, and established a firm of his
> own. He put out the volo board, a species of Ouija.
> Colonel Bowie, one of the partners, entered suit—the
> original company held the patents. . . . [Kennard] was
> forced out of the talking-board business.
>
> Some time later William Fuld, a shop foreman,
> took charge of the Ouija business, paying Colonel
> Bowie a royalty. He associated his brother Isaac with
> him. They quarreled. Isaac Fuld established the
> Southern Novelty Company and placed the Oriole
> Talking board on the market. In 1915 William Fuld
> held the United States patent, two United States
> trademarks, three Canadian trademarks, a Canadian
> patent, and the United States copyright on the name
> "Ouija."[16]

In 1920 Colonel Washington Bowie, a former partner in
the Kennard Novelty Company, testified that there were two
other possible contenders for the invention of the board: E. C.
Reichie and C. W. Kennard. According to Bowie, Reichie was
a cabinetmaker living in Chestertown, Maryland, in 1890. Although not a spiritualist himself, he was acquainted with
table-rapping and "noticed sympathetically that a large table
was a heavy thing for a frail spirit to juggle about [so] . . . he
devised a little table—the Ouija board." C. W. Kennard stum-
bled on "spooks and commercial possibilities" in the kitchen
of his Maryland home when he placed a saucer on the bread-
board and watched it move, "as though of its own volition."
He soon formed the Kennard Novelty Company, which produced "a little talk-table, first known as the Witch Board."[17]
The discrepancies of these accounts cannot finally be settled,
but it is clear that the name of William Fuld is historically attached to the Ouija board and its manufacture.

W. FULD.
GAME APPARATUS.

No. 479,266.   Patented July 19, 1892.

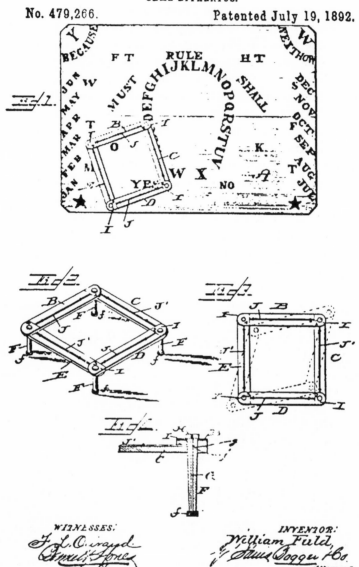

WITNESSES:

INVENTOR:
William Fuld,

Figure 3.

From his youth, William and his brother Isaac had a moderate interest in the supernatural: Fuld once told a newspaper reporter that he and his brother "had been tinkering with 'a spirit board' since they were boys, mostly for their own amusement."[18] The modern Ouija board is essentially the same as the one patented over one hundred years ago, with only minor variations. The board is rectangular, approximately eighteen inches long and twelve inches wide. The first boards were constructed of three-ply pine, but the modern ones are made of Masonite. The surface of the board is printed with the numbers zero through nine, the letters of the alphabet, the words "yes" and "no" at opposite upper corners, and the words "good bye" at the bottom (see Figure 4). The message indicator has undergone various changes: currently the small plastic table is heart-shaped, six inches long, and has three legs. It glides easily under the finger-tip touch of its operator(s). The indicator may spell out words or sentences.

Figure 4.

Fuld admitted consulting the Ouija board several times. One occasion concerned the actual naming of the device. When he was questioned about its odd name, Fuld noted that he had "asked the board to name itself, and it obliged."[19] For a while Fuld and his brother Isaac produced the game boards in their home workshop; in 1899 they occupied a small factory building at Hartford and Lamont in Baltimore.[20] For the next twenty years, the factory cranked out the boards in ever-increasing numbers. The need for more space was soon apparent, but William was conservative in his approach and seemed unsure about expanding. As he later explained to a reporter, he queried the Ouija board and it told him "to 'prepare for big business,' and on that advice I called in architects and builders and planned a factory of much greater capacity."[21] William left his job with the customs service and erected a three-story factory two blocks from his home, at a cost of $125,000.[22] Publicly, Fuld denied that the board had any special powers, emphasizing that it was created for amusement only. He once remarked: "Believe in the Ouija board? I should say not. I'm no spiritualist. I'm a Presbyterian—been one ever since I was so high."[23] But this much is clear—Fuld left his long-time job, invested heavily in a new building, and enjoyed huge profits—all at the Ouija board's prompting. He denied that he continuously conferred with the Ouija board: "I built this factory on Ouija's advice, but haven't consulted the board since then. Things have been moving along so well I didn't want to start anything."[24]

The wealth William Fuld realized from the sale of the Ouija board did not exempt him from troubles within his own family. His brother Isaac wanted to share not only in the board's fame but also in its invention, including patents and trademarks. In 1920 the brothers went to court and the local newspaper carried the details:

The courts have just finished deciding the momentous question, "Ouija, Ouija; who's got the Ouija?" as propounded in the case of Fuld vs. Fuld, William Fuld's brother Isaac being the other party to the suit. They have decided it in favor of William Fuld, making Isaac pay all the court costs and decreeing that William has the sole right to call a "Ouija" a "Ouija."[25]

It was during this trial that Colonel Washington Bowie testified about two other possible inventors: Reichie and Kennard. The court did not regard his testimony as particularly valuable and dismissed it. Bowie's testimony adds yet another curious legend to the Ouija board's mystique.

In August 1920 the Ouija board was once again the subject of a court case, this time to determine whether it was a taxable entity. Was it a game, sporting goods, or an instrument of spirit communication? The Baltimore Talking Board Company, Inc., filed a case against the Internal Revenue Service because of the tax they had levied on the company's gross income. The IRS clearly regarded the board as a game and therefore subject to the game tax. They refused to return the approximately two hundred dollars they had collected in taxes. The company took them to court.

> The company, represented by Assistant Attorney-General Allan Fisher—acting in his private capacity and not as a State official—and Col. Washington Bowie, made the contention that [the board] is a medium for communication between this world and the next and therefore does not in any sense constitute a game.[26]

It was in the company's best interests to classify the board as a toy, thus making it exempt from the exclusive game tax. In fact, a smaller version of the board was used primarily as an advertisement and was considered a toy by the company. However, the regular boards were not sold to children for their amusement but to adults for spirit communication. Both the manufacturer and the users viewed the boards more seriously. Attorney Fisher continued to impress the court with the Ouija's uniqueness. "We contend . . . that it is a form of amateur mediumship and not a game or sport. By means of this board one is enabled to get in touch with the other side."[27]

Local news reporters wanted to see a test or demonstration of the board's alleged powers right in the courtroom; this would settle the question once and for all. No such test was ever officially considered or conducted. On June 1, 1921, Judge John C. Rose handed down his decision in the United States District Court. In the words of the newspaper summary, "There is nothing of the occult or supernatural about the Ouija board, but it is simply an ordinary game, and taxable as such."[28]

This decision was clearly unacceptable to the company. In late 1921 or early 1922, it took the first of the two remaining steps in the judicial process—it filed its case with the Circuit Court of Appeals of Richmond, Virginia. The district court had little difficulty in reaching a decision, but the appellate court was divided over the nature of the Ouija board. The majority opinion, written and handed down by Judge Charles A. Woods on February 9, 1922, upheld the lower court ruling:

> It seems safe to say that psychologists recognize the Ouija board as a real means of expression of automatism. But the court cannot pretend to be ignorant that it is very largely sold with the expectation that it is to be used merely as a means of social amusement or play and is actually so used. It is true that automatism is the basis of its use, but phenomena of psychical as well as of physical nature may be the basis of amusement and games.[29]

In this ruling, the court practically conceded the company's contention about the nature of the board, but it added one of its own—namely that amusement was the basis of any game, and as such, the Ouija board was subject to taxation.

Judge Martin A. Knapp's dissenting view added an interesting twist to the case: "The Ouija board has no real likeness in construction or use to any of the specified articles. It is unique, in a class of itself."[30]

Hoping for a more favorable opinion, the company took its case to the United States Supreme Court. This last bid was short-lived. The judges simply refused to make any decision and on June 5, 1922, threw the case out of court without comment. On the following day the _Baltimore Sun_ carried an article whose title proved to be the closing comment on legal efforts to accurately define a Ouija board: "Case Over Taxes, Long Contested in Several Tribunals, Finally Thrown Out and Status of Board Remains on List of Unsolved Mysteries."[31] Despite the judicial indecision over the accurate definition of the Ouija board, the American public continued to purchase and use the boards in their homes.

Fuld's dramatic success was suddenly interrupted on February 24, 1927. The local newspaper reported the accident: "William Fuld, a former customs inspector who made more than $1,000,000 from his invention and sale of a 'spirit communications' board, was seriously injured today in a fall from the roof of his three-story toy factory."[32] Fuld had gone to help workmen replace a flagpole on the roof. As he was steadying himself with a pole support near the edge of the roof, it pulled loose, throwing him backwards. He was taken to a nearby hospital, but died the same day. It is ironic that Fuld, who claimed to have invented the Ouija board and who profited enormously from its sale, should die in a fall from the very building that the Ouija board had advised him to build!

After William's untimely death, Isaac apparently resumed his claim to be the board's inventor. Following Isaac's death on November 19, 1939, the following news article appeared: "Story of Ouija Board's Start Lost With Death of Inventor."[33] Reporters questioned members of Isaac Fuld's family about the board's invention, but the family either knew or could remember little.

Periods of Ouija Popularity

A survey of the board's popularity reveals some significant periods when demand peaked. About a year before the outbreak of World War I, Mrs. Pearl Lenore Curran, an ordinary housewife in St. Louis, Missouri, began an unusual Ouija board odyssey that was later well publicized and generated a renewed interest in the board. Mrs. Curran occasionally toyed with the board with her friends, but on July 8, 1913, her Ouija pointer slowly spelled out these words: "Many moons ago I lived. Again I come. Patience Worth is my name." This began a series of mysterious messages received through Mrs. Curran's Ouija board that continued until her death of pneumonia in a Los Angeles hospital on December 3, 1937.[34] I have summarized the principal facts of this curious case, which are as puzzling today as they were during Mrs. Curran's lifetime. The summary condenses information from several books and articles. There are at least three book-length studies written on Curran, the latest of which was published in 1972.[35]

Patience Worth claimed that she lived on a farm in seventeenth-century England and later came to America, where she died at the hands of savage Indians. Mrs. Curran was a woman of little education. "She [had] never been a student of literature, ancient or modern, and [had] never attempted any form of literary work. She [had] had no particular interest in English history, English literature, or English life."[36] Yet she was able to accurately produce works dealing with these subjects. Over a twenty-four-year period, Patience produced "the astounding total of almost four million words, seven full-length books." Some of these works sold well and were even praised by distinguished critics. She wrote over five thousand "poems ranging from a few lines in length to hundreds, uncounted numbers of epigrams and aphorisms, short stories, a few plays, and thousands of pages of witty, trenchant conversation with the hundreds of guests who came to call on her."[37] Mrs. Curran reached speeds of three thousand words an hour on the Ouija board. She discarded the board on February 12, 1920, and reached speeds of one hundred and ten words a minute in direct dictation. Eventually she learned to speak for Patience through the typewriter.[38] "On one occasion a chapter [of a novel Patience was dictating] was lost, but two months later she redictated it, and when the lost pages later came to light she was found to have repeated the identical words."[39] The dictations were accompanied by "no ceremony . . . , no dimmed lights, no compelled silences, no mummeries of any sort."[40] "Mrs. Curran was never blotted out by the personality of Patience Worth."[41] "The actual source of the Worth-Curran literary output remains unknown."[42] Patience Worth has never been identified from any historical records.

The story of Patience and Mrs. Curran intrigued a great many people and Ouija board sales soared. When Mrs. Curran abandoned the board for direct dictation, she remarked, "I hate to do this, for think of the check there will be upon the sale of Ouija boards!"[43]

Following the close of World War I, the Ouija's popularity reached new heights, thus fulfilling its predictions of "big business" to William Fuld. In December 1919, an article in the *New York Times* announced reports from several stores "of an unprecedented demand for and sale of what used to be called the planchette and now goes under the name of the Ouija board."[44] Apparently many people bought the board hoping to communicate with the spirits of soldiers killed in France. The *Times* editorialized, "It is the duty of all who know the facts as to Ouija boards to make them known to others and to denounce the misuse of the thing as a crime against intelligence."[45] During the Fuld brothers' lifetimes, 1920 was probably the record year for sales of Ouija boards—William Fuld reportedly told a friend that he had sold some three million boards.[46] The *Baltimore Sun* even "had a regular Ouija editor to answer the flood of questions it received."[47]

The Ouija board fad or craze began to spread to college campuses. The *New York Times* (January 14, 1920) carried an article on the use of the Ouija board on the Ann Arbor campus of the University of Michigan.

> Having created a national industry which bids fair to rival that in chewing gum, the Ouija board is now developing a new form of nervous prostration. From various seats of learning comes the report that the green tables of the undergraduate no longer clink with colored chips, having become the centre of an even more breathless suspense as "spirit" messages are spelled out. At Ann Arbor the faculty foresees a swelling of the "home" and "warned" lists unless studies are quickly resumed with a view to the approaching examinations. One professor dolefully proclaims that "the lure of the Ouija is becoming a serious national menace." Local medical authorities, meanwhile, report an increase of nervous diseases and prostrations.[48]

By the mid-1920s, interest in the Ouija board diminished. A few of its unusual cases were reported in newspapers and some of them appear in a later chapter. After the stock market crash of 1929, the Baltimore Talking Board Company (now operated by Fuld's two sons, William A. and Hubert) was once again producing large quantities of boards to meet the demand. A *Baltimore Sun* reporter observed that the board always sold best "in times of stress—wars, depressions, recessions."[49]

The next period of national stress, World War II, predictably produced another period of brisk board sales. In May 1944, William A. Fuld (the son) claimed that orders were pouring in so fast he couldn't get enough materials to fulfill them. When questioned about the boom, he remarked: "All I know is they [the boards] must work some time or we wouldn't be selling so many. For the last 18 months the sales have been as large as during the best years of the 20's."[50] One Baltimore bookstore alone sold over eight hundred boards a week! The "most eager purchasers [were] WACs, schoolgirls,

and office workers."[51] Large stores were even more successful; one department store in New York sold more than fifty
thousand Ouija boards in four months "to credulous and in-
credulous customers." The year before they had sold only a
few.[52] Fuld explained the revival of interest in two ways: "We
have done a lot of missionary work on it through the years
[he did not elaborate on this], and, of course, it is the times
also. In times like these people take up things like the Ouija
to find out what their sons and husbands are doing on the
other side [presumably meaning overseas]."[53]

In 1945 the magazine _Popular Science_ contained plans for
constructing a low-cost Ouija board in the home workshop[54]—
yet another indication of the board's popularity. In 1959 a _Bal-
timore Sun_ reporter learned that a certain amount of secrecy
now surrounded the board's manufacture. The Fuld brothers
no longer provided information on the number of boards sold
or the new location of its factory. The factory was moved because groups of curious visitors hampered plant operations.
People who had questions about the board had to mail them
to the company and received only written responses.[55]

The occult revival that began in the 1960s seemed certain
to produce an increased demand for Ouija boards, so Parker
Brothers, a well-known game manufacturer in Salem, Massachusetts, decided to acquire this potential gold mine. On
February 23, 1966, Parker announced that "it had acquired full
ownership of William Fuld, Inc."[56] In the same release the
president of Parker Brothers said that the company planned
"to increase production of Ouija boards by more than 100 percent over 1965 levels."[57] His anticipation of market demand
proved correct because in 1967 Ouija sales topped those of
Monopoly®—2.3 to 2.1 million.[58] John Godwin, in his book
Occult America, estimated that between 1967 and 1972 "approximately ten million of these boards have been sold, making them a $50,000,000 business and assuring that a basic min-
imum of 20 million Americans have played with them."[59]

Although some of these figures may be inflated, it is apparent that Ouija board sales and use are significant. Godwin

noted the striking new feature of this revival: "The usual wives, mothers and sweethearts of servicemen were joined by millions of teenagers, right down to the thirteen-year-old level, who had never previously shown much interest in these gadgets."[60]

If sales figures are an indicator of popularity, one might conclude that interest in the Ouija board declined during the 1970s: Russell Chandler reported sales over 400,000 in 1973;[61] in 1979 the sales for the previous decade were reported at seven million.[62] But interest in the Ouija board and the occult remains strong—books with information on the board continue to appear. The latest of these was advertised as "The first book to take a hard look at the phenomenon called 'the Ouija board.'" It was published by Barnes and Noble in 1985 and is entitled: *Ouija: The Most Dangerous Game*.[63]

Why has the Ouija board been so popular? Why have millions of people consulted it? According to a nationwide survey taken by Stoker Hunt in 1983, over 30 percent used the board to contact the dead and about the same number used it to contact the living. "The rest attempt to reach non-human 'intelligences' (spirits, angels, pets, etc.) or try to find lost objects or attempt to develop their own psychic powers. And some people go the Ouija board for guidance."[64] Guidance questions relate to such matters as career, marriage, investments, gambling, health, and even diet.[65] Perhaps the Ouija board has been popular because, in some way, it works!

Other aspects of modern Ouija board history will appear in subsequent chapters, including its role in launching the current channeling phenomenon and as the source of the books by the award-winning writer Chelsea Yarbro, who compiled the Ouija messages from "Michael" in three books: *Messages from Michael* (1979), *More Messages from Michael* (1986), and *Michael's People* (1988). We will also examine in greater detail the place of the board in teenage occult experimentation.

This historical account of the Ouija board's invention and rise to popularity proves that it is a far more complex and serious subject than is commonly understood.

Notes

1. John Godwin, _Occult America_ (Garden City: Doubleday, 1972), 271.
2. "Ouija, Ouija, Who's Got the Ouija?" _The Literary Digest_ (July 3, 1920): 66.
3. Nandor Fodor, "Ouija Board," _Encyclopedia of Psychic Science_ (New Hyde Park, N.Y.: University Books, 1966), 270. In my research for this book, I discovered a number of devices and inventions used for spirit communication or channeling and psychic purposes. Some are variations of the Ouija board, and others operate by a similar principle. Patent attorney Edward D. O'Brian spent about five years investigating what he identified as psychographs, locating over one hundred patents and about the same number of instruments. These demonstrate the ingenuity of the inventors in their attempts to explore the psychic or spirit realms. Some inventors classified their device as a "game" or as a "talking board," while others used more occult names, such as: "spirit wheel," "fortune telling device," "spiritualistic communication device," and "Swami board."
4. George McHargue, _Facts, Frauds, and Phantasms_ (New York: Doubleday, 1972), 10.
5. Ammianus Marcellinus, _The Roman History of Ammianus Marcellinus,_ trans. C. D. Yonge (New York: Bell, 1894), 505–11.
6. C. J. S. Thompson, _The Mysteries and Secrets of Magic_ (New York: Causeway, 1973), 148.
7. Epes Sargent, _Planchette; or, the Despair of Science_ (Boston: Roberts Brothers, 1868), 397–98.
8. Allan Kardec, _Experimental Spiritism,_ trans. Emma A. Wood (New York: Weiser, 1970), 196–200.
9. William Howels, _Primitive Man and His Religions_ (Garden City, N.Y.: Doubleday, 1948), 75.
10. Hans Holzer, _ESP and You_ (New York: Hawthorn, 1966), 75. Sargent also noted that: "according to Huc, the Catholic missionary, table-rapping and table-turning were in use in the thirteenth century among the Mongols, in the wilds of Tartary" (Sargent, _Planchette,_ 397).
11. William O. Stevens, _Psychics and Common Sense_ (New York: Dutton, 1953), 160–61; Holzer, _ESP,_ 75; Kardec, _Spiritism,_ 183–86. The practice of table-tipping is essentially the same today.
12. Lewis Spence, "Planchette," _The Encyclopedia of Occultism_ (New Hyde Park, N.Y.: University Books, 1960), 324; Ann Braude, _Radical Spirits_ (Boston: Beacon Press, 1989), 24–25.
13. Sargent, _Planchette,_ 1. A Chinese version of the planchette was being used before its invention in France, and "in Ningpo, in 1843, there was scarcely a house in which this mode of getting messages from the spirits was not practiced" (Spence, "Planchette," 398).

14. To my knowledge, Stoker Hunt is the first author to attribute the invention to Elijah Bond (*Ouija: The Most Dangerous Game* [New York: Barnes and Noble, 1985], 5). Parker Brothers, however, attributes the invention of the Ouija board to William Fuld as did Fuld himself.

15. Patent No. 479,266. The patent application states: "My invention relates to the improved construction of the moveable table or pointer. . . . As above stated, the construction of this board forms no part of my invention, and the nature as well as the arrangement of the words printed thereon are entirely arbitrary."

16. "Ouija," *The Literary Digest* (July 3, 1920): 68.

17. Ibid., 66. C. W. Kennard was issued a patent (No. 462,819) on November 10, 1891 on a "Talking Board" that differs from the conventional Ouija board in that the pointer is attached to a fixed pivot at one end.

18. *Baltimore Sun,* May 18, 1944, evening edition.

19. *Baltimore Sun,* May 17, 1959, morning edition.

20. *Baltimore Sun,* May 18, 1944, evening edition.

21. *Baltimore Sun,* Nov. 19, 1939, morning edition.

22. *Baltimore Sun,* July 4, 1920, morning edition; May 17, 1959, morning edition.

23. *Baltimore Sun,* July 4, 1920, morning edition.

24. *Baltimore Sun,* Nov. 19, 1939, morning edition.

25. *Baltimore Sun,* July 4, 1920, morning edition.

26. *Baltimore Sun,* Mar. 4, 1921, evening edition.

27. *Baltimore Sun,* Feb. 10, 1922, evening edition. The article refers in part to the district court trial of 1921.

28. *Baltimore Sun,* June 2, 1921, morning edition.

29. *Baltimore Sun,* Feb. 10, 1922, morning edition.

30. Ibid.

31. *Baltimore Sun,* June 6, 1922, morning edition.

32. *Baltimore Sun,* Feb. 24, 1927, evening edition.

33. *Baltimore Sun,* Nov. 20, 1939, morning edition.

34. Irving Litvag, *Singer in the Shadows: The Strange Story of Patience Worth* (New York: Macmillan, 1972), 239.

35. Casper S. Yost, *Patience Worth: A Psychic Mystery* (New York: Holt, 1916); Walter Franklin Prince, *The Case of Patience Worth* (Boston: Boston Society for Psychical Research, 1927); Litvag, *Singer in the Shadows.*

36. Yost, *Patience Worth* as cited in *Communicating with the Dead,* ed. Martin Ebon (New York: New American Library, 1968), 75.

37. Litvag, *Singer,* 2–3.

38. Ibid., 190–91, 199.

39. Rosalind Heywood, *Beyond the Reach of Sense* (New York: Dutton, 1959), 92.

40. Yost, *Patience Worth,* cited in Ebon, Communicating, 66.

41. Robert Somerlott, *"Here, Mr. Splitfoot": An Informal Exploration into Modern Occultism* (New York: Viking, 1971), 146.

42. Ibid., 147.
43. Litvag, *Singer*, 199.
44. *New York Times*, Dec. 24, 1919, p. 12.
45. Ibid.
46. *Baltimore Sun*, May 17, 1959, morning edition.
47. *Baltimore Sun*, May 18, 1944, morning edition.
48. *New York Times*, Jan. 14, 1920, p. 8.
49. *Baltimore Sun*, May 17, 1959, morning edition. William A. Fuld (son of the original owner) received a patent on the Ouija board design in use today (Patent No. 114,534, May 2, 1939). He was issued another patent on what appears to be a conventional Ouija board planchette, but with the addition of battery-powered illumination (Patent No. 1,870,677, Aug. 9, 1932).
50. *Baltimore Sun*, May 18, 1944, morning edition.
51. Ibid.
52. Gertrude Berger, "The Ouija Comes Back," *New York Times Magazine* (Sept. 10, 1944): 46.
53. *Baltimore Sun*, May 18, 1944, evening edition.
54. *Popular Science*, Feb. 1945, p. 161.
55. *Baltimore Sun*, May 17, 1959, morning edition.
56. *New York Times*, Feb. 24, 1966, p. 50.
57. Ibid.
58. Evelyn Cuoco, letter to the author, May 5, 1992. This was the only year that this was true.
59. Godwin, *Occult America*, 271.
60. Ibid., 272.
61. *Los Angeles Times*, Feb. 17, 1974, p. 1.
62. Gina Covina, *The Ouija Book* (New York: Simon and Schuster, 1979), 104. In response to my request for Ouija sales figures for the past decade, Parker Brothers Consumer Relations Advisor Evelyn Cuoco advised me that this was "proprietary information and not available to the public" (letter to the author, May 5, 1992).
63. The accuracy of this statement might be questioned as my 191-page book, *The Ouija Board: Doorway to the Occult* (Moody Press, 1975) took a "hard look" at the Ouija board. Although the Barnes and Noble publication by Stoker Hunt contains warnings on board use and contains many interesting details, it is not written from a Christian perspective and even contains two chapters on how to work the board.
64. Hunt, *Ouija*, 9.
65. Ibid., 9; Covina, *Ouija Book*, 84–87.

3

The Operation and Interpretation of the Board

Some of the most controversial aspects of the Ouija board concern the questions: What makes it work? What is the source of the messages? Are the communications received through the board just the reflection of the operator's conscious or subconscious thought, or do they sometimes reveal contact with another dimension—the supernatural? If the latter is true, what is the evidence?

What Makes It Work?

Although the instructions for the Ouija board are so simple that they are printed on the outside of its carton, I located a number of articles and books containing information on operating the board—sometimes entire chapters. These writers consider the operation of this device a serious matter, one that must be approached with the proper attitude and motives. Instructions cover a variety of topics: room conditions and lighting, the number of people in the room, the length and frequency of the sittings, proper weather conditions, the physical and mental states of the participants, their attitude toward the "controls and communicators," the method of asking questions and recording the sessions, and the proper care of the board.[1] Certainly these authors do not view the Ouija board as a game or a toy.

The Parker Brothers instructions for the board are clear, but they do not address what makes it work. To find out if the company had an answer, I wrote Parker Brothers and received a brochure that offers no solution but simply states "How or why it works is a mystery. . . ."[2] The board's instructions warn the user to operate it in a serious manner, because "if you use it in a frivolous spirit, asking ridiculous questions, laughing over it, you naturally get undeveloped influences around you." What are these "undeveloped influences" around the person(s) operating the board?

Outside of conscious manipulation, there are at least three basic explanations of what makes the Ouija board work. The first view maintains that imperceptible muscular movements cause the message indicator to move. This means that the messages come from the subconscious mind(s) of the operator(s). The second view holds that although most messages come from the subconscious, a small percentage originate from contact with disincarnate spirits or other intelligences. In certain individual cases, all messages may result from outside sources. The third view also maintains that most messages originate in the subconscious, but that a small percentage reflects contact with evil spirits or demons. According to the Bible, demons are spiritual beings in league with Satan who exert an evil influence on human affairs (Luke 4:33–36; 1 Cor. 10:20; Rev. 9:20). This is my own view on the subject and one that many Christians share, although some believe that a higher percentage of Ouija board messages are demonic in origin.

Other theories of the source of Ouija communications include ESP and what Carl Jung called "the collective unconscious," the view that individuals may tap into a shared collective memory that is inborn and not derived from personal experience.[3]

Although some Christians believe in the reality of the demonic, they regard the Ouija board only as a "pseudo-occult" device and are skeptical of its supposedly supernatural dimensions. Danny Korem, a professional magician, and Dr. Paul Meier, a Christian psychiatrist, take this position in their book *The Fakers*. Korem notes: "I have never witnessed, read, or heard of a credible report of something of a supernatural nature taking place through the use of the Ouija board." And Meier agrees: "I certainly agree with Danny Korem that any results obtained from Ouija boards is from either trickery, luck, or subconscious ideomotor action."[4]

While Korem and Meier remain skeptical that the Ouija board is an occult device, both strongly urge people not to get involved with it, or if they already have, to discontinue the practice. Korem warns, "This seemingly harmless game can prove to be one of the most dangerous of the pseudo-occultic pursuits already detailed."[5]

Most researchers do not dispute that a high percentage of the Ouija's messages are spawned by the mind(s) of the operator(s). However, many authors maintain that this cannot account for *all* that takes place.[6]

Kurt Koch presents three basic attitudes on inexplicable phenomena: "the unrealistic attitude of rational 'explaining away,' the realistic stance of scientific research, and the admission of researchers that there remains an unexplainable residue."[7] He cites parapsychologists, psychologists, and others whose experiences lead them to believe in this unexplainable residue.[8] Koch quotes the eminent parapsychological researcher Rudolph Tischner in this connection: "Let us acknowledge our complete ignorance."[9] Early in his book, Koch points out that there are some thirty theories to explain the phenomenon of clairvoyance.[10] What is the significance of so many interpretations? "These many theories are, on the one hand, a symbol of the wrestling to find the element of truth in clairvoyance, on the other hand, an unmistakable symptom of the great factor of uncertainty in all rational attempts to show the meaning."[11]

Are all the messages and manifestations connected with the Ouija board adequately explained by the operator's subconscious, as some have suggested? Not according to Martin Ebon who contends that

> even the most experienced parapsychologists, psychical researchers or psychologists cannot tell you what actually goes on. Oh, sure, there is a good deal of learned talk about "emergence of secondary personality characteristics," of "multiple personalities," of "surfacing of repressed tendencies," of "dramatized complementary, compensatory or supplementary facets within the individual." The simple truth is that nobody knows what really goes on, just as nobody knows exactly how and why we dream.
>
> What we do know, however, is that it is dangerous to open doors to the subconscious without proper safeguards. That goes for hypnosis, among other things.[12]

To deny the possibility of the intrusion of the supernatural into Ouija board use is premature. As John Godwin reminds us: "The entire spectrum of automatism remains largely unexplored."[13] Both the second and third theories about the source of the Ouija board's messages agree that some board phenomena transcend the mental powers of the participants, but their explanations represent two distinctly different worldviews. The spiritualist explanation contradicts the biblical worldview, and any attempt to combine the two would completely distort the Christian faith.[14]

> The Spiritualist hypothesis, if seriously held, gravely distorts a Christian understanding of God and creation. Briefly review the teachings which we have described and note their bearing upon the major tenets

33

of the Christian faith. The foundation of conviction is transferred from the Word to the demonstration of the seance. The Scripture becomes a record of psychic phenomena. God, if He is not rejected, is at least relegated to the fringes of concern and man—living or dead—holds the center of the stage. Man becomes *per se* immortal, and his sin is no longer against God but only against his own progress. Christ becomes a practicing medium and the Atonement becomes an offense, since salvation is only by man's inherent capacity for moral and spiritual progress. Goodness is in producing happiness for ourselves and our fellows. Judgment is forgotten, a tawdry Summerland replaces Eternal Life, and there is no more hope for the Coming of the Lord.[15]

Christians cannot interpret supernatural phenomena associated with the Ouija board as manifestations of departed spirits because the Bible clearly teaches that the human spirit does not wander after death but has an immediate destination—either heaven or hades.[16] Such expressions as "at home with the Lord" (2 Cor. 5:8) or "to depart and be with Christ" (Phil. 1:23) teach that believers go to heaven after death. Jesus said to the thief on the cross, "Today you shall be with Me in Paradise" (Luke 23:43). And in John 14:2 Jesus said to his followers, "I go to prepare a place for you." The unredeemed also have a place of abode after death known as hades—"the place where the wicked dead are tormented before the final judgment."[17] In the account of the rich man and Lazarus in Luke 16, the rich man was "in Hades" (v. 23) and "there is a great chasm fixed" between the redeemed and unredeemed (v. 26).

Instead of consulting Ouija boards or mediums about the future, the Bible clearly teaches Christians to seek God and his Word: "And when they say to you, 'Consult the mediums and the spiritists who whisper and mutter,' should not a people consult their God? Should they consult the dead on behalf of the living? To the law and to the testimony! If they do not speak according to this word, it is because they have no dawn" (Isa. 8:19–20).

How many of the Ouija's communications represent contact with the supernatural realm? Most writers are vague on this point, because no one can know with certainty. Hans Holzer estimates that 5–10 percent of the cases he has investigated actually contact the supernatural realm,[18] though he personally rejects the biblical view of demons. Allen Spraggett, a student of psychic phenomena, estimates that less than 1 percent involve the supernatural.[19] What is the significance of such estimates? Even if one accepts the reality of supernatural contact, only a small percentage of Ouija board phenomena fall into this category. Therefore each reported incident must be carefully examined and interpreted.

Communication with the Supernatural Through the Ouija Board

There are several reasons why I believe the Ouija board can be a means of communication with the supernatural realm. Although the greatest number of the board's messages are a result of the conscious and subconscious mind(s) of the operator(s), the small percentage of messages that may be of demonic origin will not always prominently display outward evidence of their diabolical source. In fact, just the opposite often may be the case. Deception is at the heart of satanic working (2 Cor. 11:14; Rev. 12:9). Information that devices like the Ouija board provide often may be helpful. Although the vileness of some spirit communications reveals their demonic source, frequently messages sound moral and impressive. Invariably, however, they suffer from one fatal defect: they ignore or undermine the unique claims of biblical Christianity. The experience of Victor Ernest, a former spiritualist who later became a Christian minister, illustrates this demonic deception.

> The spirits I encountered at seances were, for the most part, very moralistic. They encouraged us not to

smoke or drink or do anything else that would harm our minds and bodies. Ministers were told to preach morality, good manners, and civic pride. . . . The spirits often talked about an ethical Jesus, but never about the Savior who died a sacrificial death for sin.

In contrast to the high moral and ethical tone of the seances at our home, I attended some where the spirits were blasphemous and sensual. Spiritualists call them earthbound demons, and they served to reinforce our conviction that the spirits at our seances were truly from God.

Only later did I realize that the blasphemous seances were another subtle trick of Satan to convince us that there were "good" spirits and "bad" spirits, and that we were indeed communicating with God at our seances. For all evil spirits are demons, fallen creatures serving Satan. Even the spirits who told us to improve ourselves morally and spiritually were doing so to gain our allegiance for themselves and keep us from God Himself.[20]

What is the evidence that the Ouija board can be used to establish contact with the supernatural realm?

Content of Messages. The content of some of the board's communications has convinced many researchers of their supernatural nature. Researchers have verified cases where the information received from the board was unknown to its operator(s). Verification is always necessary because spirits frequently provide minute details about "their" identity that upon investigation are found to be total fabrications.[21]

Sir William Barrett, an eminent physicist and psychical researcher, investigated some Ouija board experiments that yielded accurate information. At first, the control took the name Peter Rooney and fabricated information about himself, but "other messages subsequently came through another control, giving names and addresses of two persons recently deceased in England, which on investigation proved to be perfectly correct; though the names were entirely unknown to myself or any of the sitters."[22]

Hans Holzer recounts a message he received through the Ouija board with the medium Mrs. Ethel Johnson Meyers. The communication supposedly came from an American soldier killed in the Philippines during the Second World War. The board gave information about the soldier's name, rank, serial number, and his family's residence. Holzer's inquiries to the Department of Defense about the soldier were unsuccessful, but when he sent a letter to the address mentioned by the board, the family verified the identity of the soldier and that he _had_ lived and died in the war.[23]

Earlier we discussed the case of Pearl Curran, who left school at the age of fourteen and had little or no contact with people outside her neighborhood. Yet she was able to write three historical novels (_The Sorry Tale, Hope Trueblood,_ and _Telka_) and numerous other books through the Ouija board. _Telka_ is set in medieval England. A philologist who read the novel stated that some 90 percent of the words were Anglo-Saxon in origin and that none of them were later than the eighteenth century. Other reviewers found both _Telka_ and _The Sorry Tale_ (a novel about imperial Rome) to be historically accurate. Yet Mrs. Curran knew almost nothing about history, especially Roman history. What was her explanation for these books? She accepted a spiritualist interpretation—namely that a spirit control named Patience Worth, who claimed to have lived in the eighteenth century, was responsible for her board-related writing.[24]

I could cite numerous other examples of similar experiences, but the fact remains that sometimes information from the board supports an explanation of a supernatural origin.[25] One of the major participants in the "Michael" material commented, "If I had half the information on history that has come through the board, I would need three or four major degrees. . . ." "Michael's" information was checked on several occasions and was found to be accurate.[26]

Possession (Obsession) Through Use of the Board. The phenomenon of possession (some use obsession as a synonym) following an extended period of Ouija board use further supports the contention that the device may promote supernatural contact and intrusion. From a biblical point of view, possession is the result of the intrusion of the demonic into a person's personality. Demons are fallen angels with evil and depraved natures who affect their victims mentally, morally, physically, and spiritually. "Throughout the NT other noticeable characteristics of those who were demon possessed include superior or supernatural knowledge (James 2:19), the ability to foretell the future (Acts 16:16), and superior or uncontrollable strength (Matt. 8:28; 17:15; Acts 19:16)."[27]

Harold Sherman devotes an entire chapter in *Your Mysterious Powers of ESP* to the subject of the invasion of the personality by an outside entity. While he views such an entity as a disincarnate spirit and not a demon, his observations and accounts are helpful:

> For many years, and increasingly in recent times, because of the widespread interest in Ouija boards, hypnotic regression, meditation, and automatic writing, I have been hearing from men, women, and young people who have suffered an invasion of their minds by thoughts and feelings so foreign to their natures as to cause them great concern and often panic. While many doctors and psychiatrists might dispute my interpretation, it is my conviction, based on years of research and experimentation in extra-sensory perception, that quite a number of these distressed people have become unwitting or unwilling victims of obsession or possession.[28]

After quoting actual letters from people who had experienced such invasion, Sherman commented: "There you have it—those are graphic cases that should indicate to anyone but the most closed-minded of persons that possession can be a very real phenomenon."[29] Sherman disclosed that in the few hundred cases he had examined, "the majority who have become involved with possessive and other spirit entities came by this experience through the Ouija board and/or automatic writing."[30]

Automatic writing may result from Ouija board use or lead to it. Such writing can be defined as "writing done in a dissociated state of varying degree. The writing is done without conscious muscular effort or mental direction."[31] This is the most common form of automatism and usually reflects the participant's subconscious thoughts, although on occasion an outside intelligence may intrude and operate through the writer. Sometimes the Ouija board will instruct users to get a pencil and paper. The person's arm and hand may twitch or experience a tingling sensation, then become rigid and begin to write. The person may even go into a trance-like state. Sometimes the automatic writer progresses to automatic typewriting, "inner ear communication," or even actual vocalization. Whether automatic writing results solely from the subconscious or some other agency, it can become a compulsive drive that damages the practitioner physically, mentally, and spiritually.

In 1972 Hugh Lynn Cayce (President of the Association for Research and Enlightenment [A.R.E.] in Virginia Beach, Virginia) wrote that he received "countless letters from a great many people who are having serious difficulties as a result of trying Ouija boards and automatic writing."[32] I examined some of these letters in the A.R.E. files and verified that many of these "serious difficulties" were identical to Sherman's cases of possession. I wrote the A.R.E. in 1992 to confirm if Cayce's statement was still true. The response was in the affirmative.[33]

Tests of the Ouija Board. Skeptics like Milbourne Christopher view the Ouija board solely as a device to record the conscious or subconscious mind of the operator. Such skeptics often propose tests to demonstrate whether the mind of the operator or another intelligence is at work. Christopher suggested using a randomly arranged alphabet that the sitters never see because they are not allowed to look down at the board. An even more foolproof test would involve covering the heads of the participants with a special box that would make it impossible for them to see the board. Christopher predicted that "pure gibberish will be spelled out under these conditions."[34]

Sir William Barrett performed a number of tests almost identical to those suggested by Christopher and recorded the results in the September 1914 *Proceedings of the American Society for Psychical Research*.[35] In his paper Barrett explained the experiments' background and the conclusions he reached. He reported that the Ouija board worked even when the operators were blindfolded, the alphabet rearranged (while the sitters were blindfolded), and when the surface of the board was hidden from the operators by an opaque screen.[36] Sir William noted that in one experiment the interposition of an opaque screen did stop the movement of the indicator, but that earlier the presence of the screen had made no difference. One person who was present at this experiment wrote:

> When present with Sir Wm. Barrett at the sitting in question, I observed that the interposition of the opaque screen made no appreciable difference in the speed at which the message was spelt out, and certainly it caused no interruption, much less a cessation of the message. . . . So far as I could judge the blindfolding of the sitters was perfect and their *bona fides* [were] to me beyond question. When the opaque screen was held over the board, the letters were visible only to the reporters who bent down to see underneath the screen.[37]

In his conclusion on these experiments, Barrett remarked:

I myself am absolutely convinced after careful investigation, that none of the sitters could use their normal vision, consciously or unconsciously, in the experiment recorded in this paper. We all know, it is true, the wonderful powers exhibited by the subnormal self, and many remarkable illustrations of this, and of the unconscious perception of sensory stimuli that lie below the threshold of sensation are given in our Proceedings. But I do not know of any cases which are quite parallel to these Ouija board experiments. For we have here, in addition to the blindfolding of the sitters, the amazing swiftness, precision and accuracy of the movements of the indicator, spelling out long and intelligent messages, not only without halting or error, but with emphasis on particular words, proper punctuation and the use of quotation marks in appropriate places. Messages often contrary to the expectation and beyond the knowledge of the sitters, and also the interjection of opprobrious epithets wholly foreign to the desire or habit of thought of any present.

Reviewing the results as a whole I am convinced of their super-normal character and that we have here an exhibition of some intelligent disincarnate agency, mingling with the personality of one or more of the sitters and guiding their muscular movements.[38]

Barrett includes a section of this report in his book _On the Threshold of the Unseen_ (chap. 14), where he states, "Whatever may have been the source of the intelligence displayed, it was absolutely beyond the range of any normal human faculty."[39]

In _There Is a Psychic World_ a minister records similar experiments conducted with his eleven-year-old child working the Ouija board. The girl operated the board successfully with her eyes blindfolded and with the letters of the alphabet upside down and completely rearranged on the homemade board.[40]

Hester Dowden (Mrs. Travers Smith), automatist and

psychic researcher, was known for her blindfolded operation of the Ouija board. In *Voices from the Void: Six Years' Experience in Automatic Communications,* she frequently mentions working the board blindfolded and using other tests such as a rearranged alphabet.[41] How effective was the blindfolding?

> A close black satin mask was fitted for each sitter; no glimpse of the board could be had through these unless the head was tilted far back. We did not consider these masks sufficient for "test" conditions, however, so when visitors were present we wore outside our masks opaque veils of black cotton material extending from the forehead to the waist.[42]

When challenged to perform blindfolded, Darby and Joan in *Our Unseen Guest* also claimed to have successfully operated the Ouija board blindfolded with their faces turned away from the board.[43] And more recently, psychotherapist Kathryn Ridall recounts an experience where the planchette moved from letter to letter very rapidly, even though the channel was "double blindfolded."[44]

Difficult-to-Explain Ouija Phenomena. A number of Ouija board users report experiences that are difficult to explain without recourse to some source outside the sitters.

1. Users often ask for or receive a physical manifestation to verify the reality of their experience. In one case the temperature suddenly dropped about twenty degrees and a wind swept through the room with such force that paperback books blew off the bookcase and pictures blew off the walls, although the windows and doors were shut.[45] In another incident, some college girls "asked the Ouija for a 'sign.' At precisely this moment, a study light went on 'by itself,' and a cigarette flew out of the hands of one of the girls."[46] William Peter Blatty, author of *The Exorcist,* described his own experiences with the Ouija board in *I'll Tell Them I Remember You.* To investigate his experience of singing mechanical birds

(which he believed to be a manifestation of his dead mother), Blatty turned to his Ouija board. When the indicator began moving, he asked it if his mother were present and "that very instant, those birds began to sing!"[47]

2. Some sources claim that the Ouija pointer moves without the operator's hands being on it. William Stevens related an instance when this happened to a Miss Helen Myers.[48] Harold Sherman noted that this sometimes happens, though not often.[49] Gina Covina claimed: "I've seen a pointer continue to make its way across the alphabet *after* both partners had taken their fingers away. Friends of mine report Ouija pointers flying out from under their fingers to sail across the room."[50] A man heavily involved in spiritualism and the Ouija board as a college student testified that while using a homemade board "on one occasion a wine glass moved around without anyone touching it."[51] An English woman who conducted hundreds of seances on a homemade Ouija before she became a Christian wrote:

> I was frightened on only one occasion. A newcomer to the seances alleged that I was pushing the glass. Indignantly I said that I wasn't, and asked everyone present to remove their fingers from the glass. To my horror the glass whizzed around the circle of the letters violently three times before suddenly grinding to a halt in the center of the table.[52]

The last incident involved tumbler moving, which is especially popular in Europe. The late Bishop James Pike wanted to arrange an appointment with a medium to contact his recently deceased son, Jim, but Canon John Pearce-Higgins, vice-provost of Southwark Cathedral, suggested that he try tumbler moving first. He then proceeded to give directions:

> I would suggest that you sit down with another person, take an inverted wineglass and place it on a smooth surface, cut out pieces of paper with one let-

ter of the alphabet on each and place them in a semi-
circle around the edge of the table; include slips with
the words "yes" and "no" as well, and then the two
of you place your fingertips lightly on opposite edges
of the glass and see what happens.[53]

Pike commented: "I was not very enthusiastic about the
idea. It sounded for all the world like a homemade ouija
board."[54] The glass did move to the letters M, F, and B, which
made no sense, and Pike gave up this attempt at communication. "I had no intention of spending hours sitting by a coffee table waiting for a wineglass to move around. . . . It
seemed like a waste of valuable time."[55] It is surprising that
two churchmen would employ this method to make contact
with the dead.

Finally psychical researcher Hereward Carrington
writes: "There are numerous cases on record when the board
has continued to write after the hands of all the sitters have
been removed from it."[56]

3. A number of Ouija board users recount incidents
where the pointer spells out messages that seemed
incomprehensible until the operators realized that they were
written in a foreign language. Such episodes are difficult to
explain away when the operators were not adept or even acquainted with the language(s) communicated.[57] One of the
major participants in a long-term Ouija board experience
stated that to communicate the messages they had received
on the board, they would have had to speak languages unknown to any of them, "including Arabic, Chinese, and one
or two major African languages, as well as Mayan, Aztec,
and the languages of the American Indian."[58]

In the light of Ouija message content, the phenomenon of
possession, the tests to verify operator influence, and other
difficult-to-explain phenomena, I maintain that it is reason-
able to believe that the Ouija board can establish contact with
the supernatural realm. Because it does work, the partici-

pant's interest and involvement are maintained and deepened, often to his or her detriment.

Notes _____

1. Hester Travers Smith, *Voices from the Void* (New York: Dutton, 1919), 158–64; Gina Covina, *The Ouija Book* (New York: Simon and Schuster, 1979), 43–56.
2. *The Weird and Wonderful OUIJA Talking Board Set* (Salem, Mass.: Parker Brothers, n.d.), 2.
3. Rosemary E. Guiley, *Harper's Encyclopedia of Mystical and Paranormal Experience* (San Francisco: HarperCollins, 1991), 114, 183–86.
4. Danny Korem and Paul Meier, *The Fakers: Exploding the Myths of the Supernatural*, rev. ed. (Grand Rapids: Baker, 1981), 70–71. Bob and Gretchen Passantino, noted authors on the cults and the occult, warn against the fallacy of "false analogy," and refer to magicians André Kole and Danny Korem to illustrate it. The Passantinos commend Korem and Kole for exposing fraudulent paranormal phenomena and practitioners, but note:

   > Most of the psychic phenomena for which there is enough evidence to be conclusive can be shown to be either natural or trickery. However, when we start with the basis of biblical evidence, affirming the existence of immaterial powers (both good—angels, and bad—demons), then we must assume that some psychic phenomena could be demonic in origin.
   >
   > Korem and Kole both give lip service to belief in the possibility of isolated incidents involving actual demonic power. However, both assert repeatedly the faulty analogy that if they can duplicate a phenomenon through sleight-of-hand (trickery), then they thereby have proved the true source of each report of that phenomenon (Bob and Gretchen Passantino, *Witch Hunt* [Nashville: Nelson, 1990], 118).

   "We must be very careful that our explanations of supernatural phenomena do not lull people into a false complacency, a complacency that can make them vulnerable to real occultism" (Ibid., 119–20).
5. Korem and Meier, *Fakers*, 67, 70–72.
6. Allen Spraggett, *The Unexplained* (New York: New American Library, 1967), 115; Kurt Koch, *Christian Counseling and Occultism*, 5th ed. (Grand Rapids: Kregel, 1965), 204–5.
7. Ibid., 205–6.
8. Ibid., 204–5.
9. Ibid, 204.

10. Ibid., 197–204.
11. Ibid., 204.
12. Martin Ebon, ed., *The Satan Trap: Dangers of the Occult* (Garden City: Doubleday, 1976), x.
13. John Godwin, *Occult America* (Garden City: Doubleday, 1972), 273.
14. See the discussion of spiritualism in G. H. Pember's *Earth's Earliest Ages* (Old Tappan, N.J.: Revell, n.d.), 243–391.
15. Frank Bell Lewis, "The Bible and Modern Religions: Modern Spiritualism," *Interpretation* (Oct. 1957): 454.
16. For a discussion of individual eschatology and the intermediate state one might consult Millard J. Erickson, *Christian Theology* (Grand Rapids: Baker, 1985), 1167–84.
17. Peter H. Davids, "Hades," in *Encyclopedia of the Bible*, ed. Walter A. Elwell, 2 vols. (Grand Rapids: Baker, 1988), 1:913.
18. Hans Holzer, *Life After Death* (New York: Dell, 1969), 29; Hans Holzer, *ESP and You* (New York: Hawthorn, 1966), 73.
19. Allen Spraggett, *Probing the Unexplained* (New York: World, 1971), 146.
20. Victor Ernest, *I Talked with Spirits* (Wheaton, Ill.: Tyndale, 1970), 38.
21. Holzer, *Life After Death*, 121. Also related in interviews.
22. William F. Barrett, *On the Threshold of the Unseen* (New York: Dutton, 1918), 184.
23. Holzer, *ESP and You*, 73–74.
24. Irving Litvag, *Singer in the Shadows* (New York: Macmillan, 1972), thoroughly explores the Patience Worth/Curran phenomenon.
25. This is frequently stated in the published accounts I have read and in the experiences of people whom I have interviewed.
26. Chelsea Q. Yarbro, *Messages from Michael* (New York: Berkley, 1979), 45, 247–50.
27. S. E. McClelland, "Demon, Demon Possession," in *Evangelical Dictionary of Theology*, ed. Walter A. Elwell (Grand Rapids: Baker, 1984), 307.
28. Harold Sherman, *Your Mysterious Powers of ESP* (New York: World, 1969), 118.
29. Ibid., 137. The cases are cited on pp. 120–37.
30. Harold Sherman, letter to the author, Sept. 29, 1972.
31. Robert H. Ashby, *The Guide Book for the Study of Psychical Research* (New York: Weiser, 1972), 174.
32. Hugh Cayce, letter to the author, May 4, 1972.
33. Grace C. Fogg, letter to the author, May 27, 1992. Grace Fogg is an Edgar Cayce Foundation researcher.
34. Milbourne Christopher, *ESP, Seers and Psychics* (New York: Crowell, 1970), 131.
35. William F. Barrett, "On Some Experiments with the Ouija Board and Blindfolded Sitters," in *Proceedings of the American Society for Psychical Research* (Sept. 1914): 381–94.

36. Ibid., 382–85, 392.
37. Ibid., 392–93.
38. Ibid., 393–94.
39. Barrett, *On the Threshold*, 181.
40. Horace Westwood, *There Is a Psychic World* (New York: Crown, 1949), 23–24.
41. Hester Traver Smith, *Voices from the Void* (New York: Dutton, 1919), 18–24, 41–42, 76–78.
42. Ibid., 78.
43. Darby and Joan, *Our Unseen Guest* (Los Angeles: Borden, 1943), 28–31.
44. Kathryn Ridall, *Channeling: How to Reach Out to Your Guides* (New York: Bantam, 1988), 50.
45. Yarbro, *Messages*, 34. Another manifestation is described on page 35.
46. E. L. Quarantelli and Dennis Wenger, "A Voice from the Thirteenth Century: The Characteristics and Conditions for the Emergence of a Ouija Board Cult," *Urban Life and Culture* (Jan. 1973): 385.
47. William Peter Blatty, *I'll Tell Them I Remember You* (New York: Norton, 1973), 169–72.
48. William Stevens, *Psychics and Common Sense* (New York: Dutton, 1953), 164–65.
49. Harold Sherman, letter to the author, Sept. 29, 1972.
50. Covina, *Ouija Book*, 123.
51. Larry Fogg, written statement and letter to the author, Feb. 27, 1985.
52. Elizabeth J. Aydon, letter to the author, May 12, 1992.
53. James A. Pike and Diane Kennedy, *The Other Side* (Garden City, N.Y.: Doubleday, 1968), 102.
54. Ibid.
55. Ibid., 102–3.
56. Hereward Carrington, *The Problems of Psychical Research* (New York: Dodd, Mead, 1921), 249.
57. Stevens, *Psychics*, 164, 183, 194–96. Litzka R. Gibson and Walter B. Gibson, *The Mystic and Occult Arts* (West Nyack, N.Y.: Parker, 1969), 117.
58. Yarbro, *Messages*, 45.

4

Psychic Development and the Danger of Entrapment

The uninformed and naive are often drawn to the Ouija board as a game or toy, a source of innocent fun. This initial impression is fostered by Parker Brothers' advertising and by the kind of stores that sell the board (drug stores, department and toy stores, and even supermarkets). Since the mid-1960s the Ouija board has become increasingly popular with young people. The *Wall Street Journal* reported that "officials of F.A.O. Schwarz, the New York toy store, say youngsters are big buyers of the board. Teenagers often ask the Ouija about their dates and the school exams, sales people say."[1]

To verify the Ouija board's attraction for young people, I conducted personal interviews and surveys of my college classes in 1972, 1985, and 1992. Approximately 95 percent of these students knew about the board, and many had dabbled with it—some were even more seriously involved. More than half the students indicated that they had friends, parents, or relatives who had used the Ouija board.

The public is seduced into using the board by promises

that it will enable them to explore their subconscious, to communicate with the departed, or to channel human or nonhuman spirit guides. Some participants who use the board for such purposes experience serious difficulties. Use of the Ouija board or similar devices may result in psychic "development." From a Christian viewpoint, such an "advance" is spiritually unhealthy because of the danger of occult entrapment. The more users try to develop their psychic powers and experience supernatural phenomena, the greater the likelihood that they will become dependent on the board. If a spirit guide is contacted, this dependency strengthens the guide's hold over the operator. When the control is serious, the user has little or no power to operate independently, to close out suggestions or voices, or to resist attacks. Serious participants may find they no longer need the board to hear or vocalize messages. The last stage of serious Ouija board use may result in *possession*. Users may advance relatively quickly from seemingly innocuous use of the board to possession.

Raupert and Ebon on Psychic Development and Entrapment

John Godfrey Raupert's excellent article "The Truth About the Ouija Board," written during a previous spiritist revival, clearly explains the nature of psychic development and entrapment. Raupert, a member of the Society for Psychical Research, wrote his treatment after first-hand investigation and acquaintance with the subject. Although the article was published in 1918, it is just as relevant today as when it first appeared. Several key sections are quoted below.

> At the beginning of the experiment and before the mind has attained any great degree of passivity the messages may be wholly normal, the slightly awakened subconscious mind becomes active and automatically and disconnectedly communicates some of the contents of its storehouse through the little board

or pencil. It may even falsely claim to be an independent personality—the spirit of a deceased friend or relative—especially if the experimenter strongly inclines to this belief and unconsciously suggests it to the subconscious mind. By far the larger proportion of the amusing messages and answers to questions with which we are all familiar are received where this moderate degree of passivity has been attained and where, as a consequence, the experimenter has no suspicion of peril or of being on dangerous ground. The board may make a flippant joke consistent with the peculiar temperament of the experimenter; it may cause surprise by telling the age and other particulars, unknown to the others, of a person present; it may perform a variety of feats causing the greatest possible amazement. And an independent intelligence may, of course, be connected with their production from the very beginning. But so long as the statements made contain no matter foreign to the mind of the experimenter and no answer to a question which might not have been projected from the subconscious storehouse, there is no *valid* reason for assuming the presence of an outside intelligence.

In proportion, however, as these experiments are continued and as the mind becomes more passive and lethargic, the phenomenon begins to change its character and imperceptibly to pass from the natural into the preternatural. While subconscious automatic activity continues, a message is jerked in here and there which is of a startling character and which is often seen at once to be no part of the experimenter's own mental outfit. Events taking place at a distance are accurately reported and commented upon. Disclosures are made respecting the character and doings and intimate personal affairs of persons known only to the experimenter. Messages are given, clearly and conclusively indicating knowledge and information wholly beyond the reach of the writer's own mind. And they are conveyed in a form and manner suggesting the presence of a critical and observant mind and of a judgment quite at variance with that of the experimenter.

When, in view of such astonishing communications, further questions are asked, the answer is generally to the effect that the spirit of some deceased friend or relative of the experimenter is present, that he has found this simple means of communication, and that he is anxious to cultivate the intercourse thus established for the benefit of the experimenter and the human race at large. For is it not a blessing of the highest order, it is urged, to obtain evidence that the dear departed dead are certainly alive and are all around us; and is it not perfectly lawful for us to receive from them advice and direction, not only as regards some of the greater problems of life, but also respecting our more immediate temporal concerns and anxieties? After a while instruction is generally given how a greater degree of passivity can be attained and how this mode of intercourse between the worlds seen and unseen can be made more perfect and profitable.

The experimenter, fascinated by these communications and convinced that he has come upon a great and valuable discovery, readily adopts the advice given and resorts to the Ouija board habitually and systematically. Any doubt expressed by others as to the *true* source of the messages or the character and integrity of the spirits operating is brushed aside with a smile of contempt, seeing that the messages breathe nothing but kindness and benevolence and that harm cannot be expected to be worked by a deceased mother or sister or friend. . . .

Communication with the "friends" of the unseen world now becomes the one exciting and all-absorbing interest and occupation, to which all other duties and interests are subordinated.

In proportion as physical vigor, and therefore the power of resistance and of will decline, and passivity and apathy increase, the spirit gains closer access to the mind, directs and influences its operation and, in the course of time, gets complete control of it. When this control has been effected and the power of resistance has been quite broken down, the mind becomes more and more susceptible to suggestion and less and less able to exercise with regard to it a discriminating and controlling power. The messages then come with great regularity and conciseness and immediately [when] the experimenter touches the board; but their moral tone is seen to have undergone a very great change. From the normal and healthy mind's point of view they are distinctly immoral and mischievous in their aim and character. They may refer to a husband or a wife whose loyalty is questioned, or they may throw suspicion upon the motives prompting the action of friends or relatives, especially if they happen to object to these experiments. Or, in the case of young people, the message may hint that the established laws of morality are, after all, only conventional laws, framed by man, and that it is not necessary to be so strict—that certain instincts imparted to human nature were imparted by God and may be lawfully obeyed, and that a time has come when men must not allow themselves to be enslaved by these old-time fetters any longer. The Christian law is ridiculed and Christian customs and practices are declared to be old-fashioned and out of date.

These suggestions are made in the most subtle manner, in exalted language, appealing to the youthful imagination and to dangerous tendencies latent in all men; and when it is borne in mind that the invisible counsellor who makes these suggestions is believed to be a kindly father or mother who could only desire the well-being of her child, and that the experimenter's power of discrimination is lost, one can imagine how far this kind of mischief can be carried.

As the "psychic development" advances, the entire mental and moral nature of the experimenter becomes disordered; and he discovers to his cost that, while it was an easy thing for him to *open* the mental door by which the mind could be invaded, it is a difficult, if not an impossible thing, to *shut* that door and to expel the invader. For the impulse to communicate or to write now asserts itself imperatively and incessantly, at all hours of the day and in the midst of every kind of occupation and, in the end, even at night, either suddenly awakening the victim or preventing him from securing any refreshing sleep. A pitiable condition of mental and moral collapse, often terminating in suicide or insanity, is frequently the ultimate result.[2]

In his introduction to *The Satan Trap: Dangers of the Occult,* well-known author Martin Ebon presents a more recent overview of such phenomena.

It all may start harmlessly enough, perhaps with a Ouija board or, one step further, with "automatic writing." The cases are mounting up where men or women follow such "messages" with slave-like obedience. . . .

The Ouija board fad shows a general pattern. Someone will start playing with it "for kicks," and others will join in, with general hilarity. . . . The Ouija will often bring startling information, telling things that "only I knew," establishing credibility or identifying itself as someone who is dead.

It is common that people who get into this sort of game think of themselves as having been "chosen" for a special task. The Ouija board will often say so, either directly or by implication. It may speak of "tests" that the sitters must undergo to show that they are "worthy" of this otherworldly attention. . . . Quite often the Ouija turns vulgar, abusive or threatening. It grows demanding and hostile, and sitters may find themselves using the board or automatic writing compulsively, as if "possessed" by a spirit, or hearing voices that control and command them.

This is no longer rare. I'd say it is now so frequent as to be common.[3]

Cases of Psychic Development and Entrapment

To illustrate how seeking psychic development or spirit guides through the Ouija board can lead to entrapment, we shall examine several actual experiences of Ouija users. Harold Sherman records several instances where psychic progress (entrapment) led to personality invasion,[4] through either automatic writing or the Ouija board. Sherman summarizes some characteristics of entrapment:

It is communication, starting under the guise of spiritual and philosophic messages, strongly appealing to the sensitive people receiving them, and then either subtly or abruptly changing to profane and obscene writings, or "direct voicings" and sensual feelings of such a revolting nature as to terrorize those so influenced.[5]

Sherman points out that these users were people of intelligence, education, culture, character, and refinement.[6] In one account, he tells of a young girl whose boyfriend was killed in an auto crash. Her first attempt to contact him through the Ouija board seemed immediately successful. The contact claimed to be the dead young man and this encouraged the mother, daughter, and her sister to work the board for hours. The mother began to suspect that the spirit was only pretending to be the young man because some messages had evil overtones. The mother writes:

> We kept on with it, though, and automatic writing was suggested. I sat down one night and started writing in a strange hand, not my own. I remember the first sentence was, "I am a new spirit from hell." It frightened me, but I kept on writing. . . .
>
> We also found that we were able to make things move . . . by resting our fingers on them, not pushing; some other force was doing it. . . .
>
> My daughter told me about her hands and arms starting to move one night after she went to bed. . . .
>
> I also noticed my arms and hands moving after I went to bed. In the meantime, the messages began to frighten me more and more, such as "M.R. is partly in your mind." Whenever we used the board, the spirit identified itself as "M.R."
>
> One night, after some more automatic writing, I thought that I heard a faint voice; as my daughters spoke to me, this voice would answer in my mind. . . . Later I was "told" that I could hear the voice all the time, but the entity preferred writing. . . .
>
> I was not able to sleep much anymore, as this entity, or "whatever it was," kept communicating all the time, for hours.
>
> The horror grew steadily worse . . . but what I couldn't understand . . . I was never tired or sleepy the next day after a sleepless night. There came a night, however, when I didn't sleep at all, and around five in the morning, the voice became harsh and loud and started to curse. . . .
>
> . . . After I had shut this thing out of my mind, I went to bed a few nights later and was prevented from sleeping the entire night. I was subjected to the most powerful sexual stimulation that I had ever known, and I could do nothing to stop it. . . .

On Palm Sunday morning, I awakened, and again I was experiencing this sexual stimulation. My body was turning violently from one side to another. Then I was on my back, and it was as if I was being attacked, only there was not anyone there—that I could see.

I started praying again, and it stopped.[7]

This account provides a fairly typical example of what can happen when the Ouija board is used seriously.

The next case comes from the correspondence files of the Association for Research and Enlightenment that I was permitted to read. This woman wrote:

About four months ago the strangest months of my life ended, and the last three of those four months had been the most nerve racking and frightening.

. . . I should tell you how this all began. I borrowed a Ouija board for a party and asked if I might keep it for two weeks just to play with it.[8]

She discovered that she could work the board alone with a spirit control named Phoebe who became dominant.

Within a week I was able to talk very rapidly and to receive messages rapidly. . . .

. . . At the end of two weeks when I was to return the board Phoebe told me I could converse with her by merely saying the words in my mind and listening for the answers.

. . . From this time on I was enmeshed in a world of spirits. And they were by no means all "angelic."

As I said my prayers there was a running translation going on a fraction of a second after my words and with an entirely different meaning. I was sure they were trying to break my pattern of prayer and

they did it to such an extent for several days I could
not pray at all and was almost into their power. . . .
Had I not had implicit trust in our Heavenly Father
and had He not taken over my survival, I think my
mind might not have withstood those attacks.

The several dozen letters in the A.R.E. files that I was
allowed to read all shared similar patterns of development
and entrapment. In 1956 Hugh Lynn Cayce received letters
from 274 people who had encountered serious problems because of automatic writing or Ouija board use.[9] By 1972
Cayce was still receiving numerous letters from people who
had "serious difficulties as a result of trying Ouija boards and
automatic writing." In 1992 Edgar Cayce Foundation researcher Grace Fogg confirmed that Cayce's statement "is
still true today."[10]

This next account typifies Ouija board users who share a
spiritualist worldview and accept the Ouija's messages as
genuine communications from the supernatural realm. Mrs.
Doris Buckley explains how she and her husband, Dan,
joined the Theosophical Society in 1946 but later dropped out
because of busy schedules. After moving from California to
Oregon, they met several men who were interested in occultism, mysticism, and metaphysics. This circle became the
nucleus for a discussion and study group.

In June 1956 a friend of one of the discussion group
members asked the Buckleys: "Have you ever tried using a
Ouija board?" The Buckleys admitted using the board in the
past, but now it was in the attic and its pointer was missing.
The couple retrieved the board and substituted a silver dol-
lar for the pointer. Dan and his friend began working it. Mrs.
Buckley recorded their experiences over the next few weeks
and the "progress" they made.[11]

There were a few random remarks spelled out on it
while they were getting the feel of it. Then short mes-

sages came directed at those of us present. These were remarks that indicated personal knowledge of the person spoken to. . . . Eventually, it became evident that it worked best with Dan alone on it. As it often happened that many times only he and I were present for messages, this left me free to take them down in writing.

On July 12 an entity who was to be our teacher for a time announced himself: "Walter Norton at your service. I passed over in 1937 in the country of the Scots."

We asked him a few questions about himself and then inquired if he had a message for us.

"Yes," he answered, "I suggest that Doris and her mother go to Camp New Era this weekend. This is very important."

New Era is a site of a Spiritualist camp near Portland, Oregon. . . .

We went to Camp New Era. . . . We witnessed and experienced communication with persons, or entities, who had passed from the earthly plane of living but who seemed very much alive when they talked with us through a medium. . . . With this introduction, we were better prepared to accept and use the experiences that were to come to us.

During the rest of July, we had many communications with Walter Norton on the Ouija board.[12]

On August 3, the spirit instructed them to dim the lights of the room in order for a new phenomena to take place. All the lights were turned off and only the light from the street lamp outside now lit the room.

Dan heaved a sigh, settled back in his chair, closed his eyes, and seemed to go to sleep. In a few moments, he sat upright, his eyes still closed, and began to speak in a voice that was not like his own.

"Walter Norton speaking through Dan Buckley. This will take quite a while. Dan is new at this so don't look for perfect results. Most especially, Doris should look for lights and possible manifestation of her grandmother."

. . . Later, after Dan came out of the trance, his clairvoyant sight had been opened and he could "see" my grandmother standing beside me trying to talk with me. . . . I couldn't see or hear her.

From that time on, other teachers came to us, sometimes on the Ouija board, sometimes in [a] trance. Dan usually started with the board and then slipped off into [a] trance.[13]

Other "teachers" came and went. "We were given teachers from other planets in the universe . . . Saturn . . . Venus . . . Jupiter."[14]

I corresponded with a man (we'll call him Chris) who developed an interest in the occult while attending college.[15] Two of his friends who used the Ouija board claimed to see apparitions and other psychic phenomena. Although initially skeptical, Chris joined in sessions with four to six other college students and eventually witnessed spirit activity. He studied material on psychic phenomena and the literature from Duke University on ESP, which lent credibility to what he observed during the seances.

Certain group members consulted mediums who went into trances to contact the spirit world. Chris decided to try hypnosis in his quest for spiritual knowledge. One of his friends successfully hypnotized his girl friend. At first their efforts met with no success, but one night when she was in a deep trance, a strange voice announced that the spirit world was observing their experiments with great interest and encouraged them to continue. Both male and female spirits spoke and could be distinguished by their various accents and mannerisms. This method of spiritual contact is now called channeling.

Chris decided to learn hypnosis himself and then tried to hypnotize his own girl friend. He was successful on his first try. After a few weeks, he could establish contact within a few minutes and carry on lengthy conversations lasting more than an hour. The girl was often tired and emotionally upset after a session. "John," the primary spirit contact, claimed to be a distant deceased relative of the subject. Other spirit personalities (both good and bad) were eager to join the sessions, but spirits who were immoral during their mortal life were only allowed to talk occasionally. Most discussions remained on a high intellectual and moral plane. The spirit contacts explained that there was a definite spiritual hierarchy and described God as a remote and glorious light, but they never mentioned Christ, and most theological discussions were limited to reincarnation. One evening Chris conversed at length with a "recently deceased" professor of psychology whose area of expertise was schizophrenia and multiple personalities. The professor claimed such phenomena were a result of reincarnation and described how prominent historical figures such as Hitler and Stalin were part of this rebirth process.

Chris came to depend on the spirits for guidance in every area of his life. In fact he hardly made any decisions without asking their advice. The girl experienced automatic writing. The spirit in control was so strong that she was unable to stop her hand from writing even with her other one—the pencil would break or the paper would tear. One evening the girl went into a trance without Chris's hypnotizing her. "John" informed them he was taking the initiative for contact. Now "John" began to come without any outward sign, and the girl was unaware of his presence. Sometimes Chris wasn't sure who was speaking. Chris conducted seances once or twice a week for almost a year. The sessions left the girl nervous and agitated, and finally her health began to deteriorate. Consequently Chris ceased this spiritualistic activity, and eventually the strain destroyed their friendship.

Chris tried to fill his spiritual vacuum by using other mediums, but with no success. Finally God confronted Chris with the gospel and he became a Christian. Jesus now filled his emptiness with the peace and satisfaction that he vainly sought in spiritualism. As he began to study the Bible, Chris recognized the similarity of demon possession to his seance experiences. His primary motivation in sharing this unhappy episode with me was to help prevent someone else from becoming entrapped and dominated by the occult.

Alan Vaughn is a paranormal researcher, psychic, author, and, more recently, a channeler.[16] His only significant experience with the Ouija board began in November 1965 when he was the science editor for a New York textbook publisher. A confirmed skeptic, Vaughn believed that "psychic phenomena and the supernatural simply did not exist . . . [and] were nothing but the product of primitive thinking and misinterpretation of natural phenomena. . . . Further, I had never had a psychic experience nor did I know anybody who had ever had one. It was a classic case of profound ignorance."

Vaughn learned about the Ouija board from his friend Delores, who reported receiving "mysterious messages." He tried playing the board with his friend Annalene who was in the hospital, but it didn't work. After Annalene's release, they tried the board again, and this time the planchette moved rapidly in answer to their questions—responses that Vaughn claimed were beyond their knowledge. As a result, the Ouija board became his constant companion.

Vaughn invited three friends to a seance at his apartment. The contact, "Z," claimed to be a male but refused to give any other personal information. Vaughn was impressed by this contact.

> Z really did seem to be a spirit entity. And this conviction sprang more from an actual feeling I had of his presence than of his words. In some way I couldn't then explain, his essence of personality was more palpable to me than the personalities of the living peo-

ple in the room. I sensed a great rapport with him and felt comfortable in his presence. Z seemed very wise.[17]

The next day Vaughn worked the board alone and received a message from a spirit named "Nada," who provided him with a brief personal history. He was so impressed by "Nada's" strong presence that he phoned a friend to witness the event, but there was no answer. Then, Vaughn said, "I did the stupidest thing in my life. I asked Nada to come into my body and guide me to where the friend was. . . . I felt a strange sensation in my brain. A force of some sort now was uttering words I could hear in my mind."

Vaughn continued to feel "Nada's" presence as he searched for a witness. Finally he asked his girl friend Glenna to join him at the board, but it didn't work. When he tried it alone, "Nada" returned, claiming to have been Pocahontas in a previous reincarnation. Vaughn was dubious so he encouraged Glenna to operate the board alone. "Z" appeared again and warned, "awful consequences—possession." As a result of this message, Vaughn became quite frightened.

The next day Vaughn and Glenna visited their friend Harold and told him about their Ouija experiences. Although board contact was unsuccessful, Vaughn felt pressured to pick up a pencil and write "Each of us has a spirit while living. Do not meddle with the spirits of the dead. It can lead to awful consequences." Vaughn was delivered from his possession when "Nada" and "Z" were successfully expelled. Then Vaughn recounts, "I looked down again at the Ouija. I was flooded with revulsion for it. 'Destroy this thing,' I commanded. Harold obligingly threw the Ouija down an incinerator chute. And that was the end of my experimentation with the Ouija."

Although the Ouija board itself was destroyed, Vaughn remained terrified—what if "Nada" returned? He "trembled through three sleepless nights in the most abject terror [he] had ever experienced." He even wondered if he were losing his mind. As a result of his Ouija experience, Vaughn eventually studied at the Society for Psychical Research in London and later became a full-time parapsychologist. More recently, Jon Klimo notes that Vaughn "thought channeling was nonsense until 'Li-Sung' entered his life four years ago."[18]

The Ouija Board's Influence on Politics, Psychology, and Literature

The Ouija board's power and influence are not limited solely to individuals or members of occult groups. Important figures in the realm of politics, psychology, and literature have been seriously affected by their Ouija board use as the following examples will demonstrate. The importance of these figures and their movements has extended the Ouija's dominion to the general public in a number of ways, especially through the ascendancy of Alcoholics Anonymous.

Politics. Robert Somerlott, author on modern occultism, travelled extensively in Latin America and lived in Mexico. He connected the Mexican Revolution of 1910 with the use of the Ouija board.

> The Ouija has not always behaved like a toy and its effect upon the user can be unpredictable. Francisco I. Madero, who launched Mexico's major revolution of 1910 and was briefly the country's president until his assassination, had been told by the planchette that he would attain the nation's highest office—an achievement possible only through revolution. Madero subsequently led a revolt and the Diaz dictatorship was overthrown. "Patriotic" biographers have minimized the Mexican president's belief in the occult, which was obviously great.[19]

Other sources verify Madero's involvement with spiritism. Dr. Charles C. Cumberland in his book, *Mexican*

63

Revolution, Genesis Under Madero, identifies Madero "as a leader of spiritism in Mexico."[20] Hubert Herring also refers to Madero's use of spiritism.

> Mexico's redemption was overdue, but Madero proved a frail instrument. He had the assurance of tapped-out messages from the spirit world that he was foreordained to the task, but the spirits had failed to warn him that national salvation does not always attend the Australian ballot.[21]

Mackenzie King (1874–1950) held the post of prime minister of Canada longer than anyone else, his final term lasting from 1935–48. Following his death, Blair Frazer wrote an article entitled "The Secret Life of Mackenzie King, Spiritualist." King believed

> it possible to communicate with the departed, and that he himself had talked beyond the grave many times with his mother, his brother and sister, and such friends as Franklin D. Roosevelt and Sir Wilfrid Laurier. He did repeatedly attend seances and have sittings with mediums here in London and elsewhere.
>
> To his real intimates he made no secret of these beliefs. Some of them joined him many times in sessions with the Ouija board at Ottawa.[22]

King began keeping a diary in 1893, which allows researchers to reconstruct much of his private life.[23] We will cite only one of the numerous books written about him— C. P. Stacey's, *A Very Double Life: The Private World of Mackenzie King.* Stacey was a professor at Princeton and at the University of Toronto. Two of his chapters detail King's spiritualist involvement. "Readers of King's diary will find it hard to discover from it just how he and Joan [Patteson] worked the little table. He seems to have left no description of their technique."[24] Stacey finds that "King's advance into spiritualism was slow and gradual, and he cannot be said to have embraced it fully until he was fifty-eight."[25] The record from this time period onward reveals many visits to mediums for seances and many seances with the "little table."[26] On at least one occasion King visited a medium "who used a Ouija board for conversations with those in the Beyond."[27] King's level of education (a Ph.D. from Harvard) and his high political office did not exempt him from involvement with the Ouija board.

Popular Psychology. Alcoholics Anonymous (A.A.) is an international organization whose twelve-step program has been espoused by thousands of alcoholics and drug users. "The Bible of recovery groups is The Twelve Steps, a set of laws that have moral overtones but are divorced from atonement, forgiveness, justification, and the power of the Spirit. The language of codependence is the language of physical disease and health."[28] In 1951 A.A. began a support group network for the spouses of alcoholics called Al Anon, which spread their concept of codependency and the twelve-step program throughout the general population, and many groups meet in local churches. The founders of this vast movement are Dr. Bob Smith and Bill Wilson. Two biographies on the cofounders, published by Alcoholics Anonymous World Services, *Dr. Bob and the Good Oldtimers* and *'Pass It On'* reveal both men's involvement in spiritualism from the inception of the organization (1935) and in the years that followed. Chapter 16 of *'Pass It On'* provides an excellent overview of their spiritualist involvement.[29] In Bill's letters to his wife Lois "there are references to seances and other psychic events . . . during that first Akron summer with the Smiths, in 1935."[30] Bill experienced a number of contacts with the "departed." The most dramatic occurred during a visit to a friend's house on Nantucket Island in 1944, where he claims that a number of entities conversed with him. Bill claimed that this experience was not a fantasy, but actually happened because he was able to verify the past existence of three of the visitors.[31]

"As early as 1941, Bill and Louis were holding regular Saturday 'spook sessions' at Bedford Hills. One of the downstairs bedrooms was dubbed by them the 'spook room'; here, they conducted many of their psychic experiments."[32] Bill Wilson provides an account of one of his Ouija board sessions:

> The Ouija board got moving in earnest. What followed was the fairly usual experience—it was a strange melange of Aristotle, St. Francis, diverse archangels with odd names, deceased friends—some in purgatory and others doing nicely, thank you! There were malign and mischievous ones of all descriptions, telling of vices quite beyond my ken, even as former alcoholics. Then, the seemingly virtuous entities would elbow them out with messages of comfort, information, advice—and sometimes just sheer nonsense.[33]

Bill also received messages without the board. His wife describes one of these sessions:

> Bill would lie down on the couch. He would "get" these things. He kept doing it every week or so. Each time, certain people would "come in." Sometimes, it would be new ones, and they'd carry on some story. There would be long sentences; word by word would come through. This time, instead of word by word, it was letter by letter. Anne [a neighbor] put them down letter by letter.[34]

The communication in this case was in Latin, a language that Bill understood only slightly. Bill took the material to a classical scholar who read the message and was impressed by it.[35]

Bill Wilson wrote the now famous "Twelve Steps"

> while lying in bed . . . with pencil in hand and a pad of yellow scratch paper on his knee. . . . As he started to

write, he asked for guidance. And he relaxed. The words began tumbling out with astonishing speed. He completed the first draft in about half an hour, then kept on writing until he felt he should stop and review what he had written. Numbering the new steps, he found that they added up to twelve—a symbolic number; he thought of the Twelve Apostles, and soon became convinced that the Society should have twelve steps.[36]

This description of how the Twelve Steps were recorded caused one writer sympathetic to channeling to speculate, *"By this description, could it be that Bill went into his meditative state and used automatic writing to 'channel' the Twelve Steps?"*[37]

Tom was a regular at the seances and maintained that "Bill and Dr. Bob believed vigorously and aggressively. They were working away at spiritualism; it was not just a hobby. And it related to A.A., because the big problem in A.A. is that for a materialist it's hard to buy the program."[38]

Twentieth-Century American Literature. At least two well-known American authors have consulted the Ouija board to assist them in producing serious poetry: James Merrill and Sylvia Plath. Merrill's poetry is noteworthy for its volume and for his long-term involvement with the Ouija board. Plath's poetry is an outgrowth of her occult experimentation.

James Merrill and his companion David Jackson have used the Ouija board together since 1953; they "got good results . . . the first time they experimented with it."[39] Over the years a three-volume work emerged with the Ouija's help, *The Changing Light at Sandover*. This trilogy of more than five hundred pages won the Pulitzer Prize for Poetry (1976), the National Book Award (1979), and the National Book Critics' Circle Award (1983).

Written over a five-year period,

the entire poem is the record of many evenings spent by the poet and his companion David Jackson attending upon the Ouija board. "The Book of Ephraim" was composed of 26 separate but consecutive poems, corresponding to the board's alphabet from A to Z. "Mirabell: Books of Number" was divided into ten sections, corresponding to the board's numbers from zero to nine. "Scripts for the Pageant" consists of three sections, corresponding to the board's Yes and No.[40]

Helen Vendler interviewed Merrill in 1979 and describes the work and its transcription:

[These are] conversations held, via the Ouija board, with dead friends and spirits in "another world." Merrill and . . . Jackson receive the messages which are transcribed letter by letter; Merrill then edits and rewrites the transcriptions. The transcriptions are set in a frame of autobiographical narrative and personal reflection. The spirits and the dead speak in capital letters; the poet writes in lower case.[41]

During the interview, Vendler asked, "Couldn't you have written [this] without the help of the Ouija board, since it all comes out of your 'word bank'?" To which Merrill replied, "It would seem not." In response to another question about why he considered the board necessary, Merrill replied, "You could think of the board as a delaying mechanism. It spaces out, into time and language, what might have come to a saint or a lunatic in one blinding ZAP."[42]

During the month of July 1991 Merrill and Jackson set aside nine consecutive afternoons for receiving messages through the Ouija board. They conversed, usually one at a time, with a series of literary personages that included Gertrude Stein, Alice B. Toklas, Colette, Jean Genet, William Carlos Williams, Elizabeth Bowen, and Henry James. The lengthy article in *The Paris Review* that covered these sessions of Ouija activity indicates that Merrill and Jackson still consider the board very seriously, as do those members of the literary community who praise Merrill's work.[43]

Most of Merrill and Jackson's transcriptions are highly subjective and unverifiable. Their leading questions received answers ranging from theological insights, to career moves authors made in previous lives, to explicit sexual descriptions of a homosexual lifestyle (Genet's).

The fierce, tormented life and work of Sylvia Plath have been the subjects of considerable study since her death in 1963. She "was a luminous talent, self-destroyed at the age of thirty, likely to remain, it seems, one of the most interesting poets in American literature."[44] Biographers and literary critics uncovered Plath's occult experimentation and her involvement with the Ouija board in their research.

During her marriage to English poet, Ted Hughes, he once gave her a set of tarot cards for her birthday. She "believed that her horoscope indicated she should become a practicing astrologist."[45] Author Paul Anderson relates that Sylvia and "Ted had frequently read a Ouija board they had constructed from cutout letters, a coffee table, and a wineglass. Some nights, as they worked the board, they met an assortment of spirits, with names like Keva, Pan, and Jumbo."[46]

Plath and Hughes frequently experienced financial difficulties, so they decided on "a scheme to produce income centered on the Ouija board. They had recently contacted a new spirit, G.A., who assured them of his ability to predict the weekly British football pool, which had pots of up to seventy-five thousand pounds."[47] The predictions made for one Saturday's matches were all accurate, but were off by one match.

In his notes on Plath's poetry, Hughes includes an unpublished poem of nearly six hundred lines he claims she wrote using the Ouija board: "The following 'Dialogue over a Ouija Board,' which she never showed, though it must have been written some time in 1957–58, used the actual 'spirit' text of one of the Ouija sessions."[48] If this poem was not well known before 1991, it became so after the prize-winning critical essay by Prof. Timothy Materer. "Occultism as Source and Symptom in Sylvia Plath's 'Dialogue over a Ouija Board'" was published in the prestigious literary journal *Twentieth Century Literature*.[49]

It is unfortunate that both Merrill and Plath depended upon the Ouija board for some of their writing, and that their works (especially Merrill's) received such praise from the literary community.

*T*he above examples amply illustrate the dangers that await those who naively use the Ouija board to develop their psychic powers. Initially, the spirit contacts seem benign and may even offer correct information about the past and predictions about the future that eventually turn out to be true. But the nature of the communications and the spirits' hold over the operator(s) may rapidly deteriorate into frightening and vile experiences or even demonic possession. There is danger not only for the individuals directly involved with the Ouija board, but for those who are influenced by literature or movements spawned by the use of the Ouija board. Even for non-Christians, the risks seem greater than any supposed benefits.

Notes _____

1. *Wall Street Journal*, Mar. 17, 1967.
2. J. Godfrey Raupert, "The Truth About the Ouija Board," *Ecclesiastical Review* (Nov. 1918): 466–68, 474–75.
3. Martin Ebon, ed., *The Satan Trap* (Garden City: Doubleday, 1976), ix. Reprinted with permission from Doubleday.
4. Harold Sherman, *Your Mysterious Powers of ESP* (New York: World, 1969), 120–37.
5. Ibid., 119.
6. Ibid.
7. Ibid., 127–30.
8. I visited the headquarters at Virginia Beach, Virginia, in the fall of 1972. All the subsequent quotations came from a letter by Mrs. R., dated Sept. 28, 1971.

9. Hugh Lynn Cayce, "Dangerous Doorways into the Unconscious," *The Searchlight* (Apr. 1959): 6.

10. Hugh Lynn Cayce, letter to the author, May 4, 1972; Grace Fogg, letter to the author, May 27, 1992.

11. Doris H. Buckley, *Spirit Communication for the Millions* (Los Angeles: Sherbourne, 1967), 15–17.

12. Ibid., 17–19.

13. Ibid., 19–20.

14. Ibid., 20.

15. L.F., written testimony and letter to the author, Feb. 27, 1985.

16. The following summary comes from Alan Vaughn, "Phantoms Stalked the Room," Martin Ebon ed., *The Satan Trap* (Garden City: Doubleday, 1976), 155–65; also included in part in Alan Vaughn, *Patterns of Prophecy* (New York: Hawthorn, 1973), 3–5.

17. Ibid., 158.

18. Jon Klimo, *Channeling: Investigations on Receiving Information from Paranormal Sources* (Los Angeles: Tarcher, 1987), 66.

19. Robert Somerlott, *"Here, Mr. Splitfoot": An Informal Exploration into Modern Occultism* (New York: Viking, 1971), 4.

20. Charles C. Cumberland, *Mexican Revolution, Genesis Under Modero* (New York: Greenwood, 1952), 33.

21. Hubert Herring, *A History of Latin America*, 3d ed. (New York: Knopf, 1968), 339–40.

22. Blair Frazer, "The Secret Life of Mackenzie King, Spiritualist" *Macleans* (Dec. 15, 1951): 8.

23. C. P. Stacey, *A Very Double Life* (Toronto: Macmillan of Canada, 1976), 9–10.

24. Ibid., 172.

25. Ibid., 162.

26. Ibid., 167–215.

27. Ibid., 169–70.

28. Edward Welch, "Codependency and the Cult of the Self," in *Power Religion*, ed. Michael Scott Horton (Chicago: Moody Press, 1992), 222.

29. *Dr. Bob and the Good Oldtimers* (New York: A.A., 1980), 311–12; *'Pass It On,'* (New York: A.A., 1984), 275–85.

30. *'Pass It On,'* 275.

31. Ibid., 276–78.

32. Ibid., 278.

33. Ibid.

34. Ibid., 278–79.

35. Ibid., 279.

36. Ibid., 197–98.

37. Nancy Rajala, "Spirituality and the 12 Steps," *The Inner Voice* (July-Aug. 1992): 9.

38. *'Pass It On,'* 275.
39. Stoker Hunt, *Ouija: The Most Dangerous Game* (New York: Barnes and Noble, 1985), 45.
40. *Book Review Digest 1980*, 830.
41. *The New York Review of Books,* May 3, 1979, p. 12.
42. Ibid., 12–13.
43. "The Plato Club," *The Paris Review* (Spring 1992): 14–84.
44. Elizabeth Hardwick, "On Sylvia Plath," in *Ariel Ascending: Writings About Sylvia Plath,* ed. Paul Alexander (New York: Harper and Row, 1985), 100–101.
45. Paul Alexander, *Rough Magic: A Biography of Sylvia Plath* (New York: Viking, 1991), 199.
46. Ibid.
47. Ibid., 200–201.
48. Ted Hughes, ed., *The Collected Poems: Sylvia Plath* (New York: Harper, 1981), 276.
49. *Twentieth Century Literature* (Summer 1991): 131–47.

5

A Dangerous "Game"

Specialists in the occult often mention the potential dangers inherent in Ouija board use and other psychic experimentation, even though many of them encourage such involvement. These dangers are amply illustrated by users' experiences. Despite the warnings of spiritualists, psychologists, psychiatrists, medical doctors, theologians, pastors, and other informed persons about the hazards of using the Ouija board and similar devices, the general public still remains largely ignorant.

People who know nothing about the occult view the Ouija board as an innocent device and regard anyone who warns about its physical, mental, and spiritual risks as an extremist, obsessed with groundless fears. How could the use of so simple a device result in anything detrimental to the user? Usually this attitude persists until people become personally acquainted with the board's hazards.

Warnings and Psychological Danger

In *Probe the Unknown*, Raymond Bayless and William Welch refer to the Ouija board as both a "dangerous toy" and a "useful psychic tool." Interestingly, Welch is a spiritualist who argues that the Ouija is a bona fide psychographic device, yet he still warns users of the distinct dangers inherent in such psychic experimentation. Bayless urges that

> great caution should be exercised by all who wish to use the Ouija board. Yet, history shows this advice is easier given than taken. . . . But when the Ouija board and related devices are used without caution and by children, danger is close.[1]

Even some spiritualists advocate restricting the sale of the Ouija board. Bayless explains that

> so well recognized are the real dangers of indiscriminate use of the board, particularly in the case of young people, that *Psychic News,* a noted English spiritualist newspaper, in 1968 began a campaign demanding a ban on the sale of Ouija boards. I doubt that anyone would think that a spiritualistic publication encourages anything of an anti-psychic nature, but this campaign reflects a very practical awareness of the dangers of the board.[2]

In his discussion of the board as a "useful psychic tool," Welsh nevertheless admits:

> No phase of psychic experimentation is more universally maligned than the Ouija board. Unfortunately, its unsavory reputation is pretty well deserved. . . . But, because it is a relatively easy method of contacting so-called disincarnates, it is open to more abuses than any other method and subject to many more risks.[3]

Dr. Carl Wickland, a physician and director of the Psychopathic Institute of Chicago, was drawn into spiritualism and psychic research.

The serious problem of alienation and mental derangement attending ignorant psychic experiments was first brought to my attention by the cases of several persons whose seemingly harmless experiences with automatic writing and the Ouija Board resulted in such wild insanity that commitment to asylums was necessitated. . . .

Many other disastrous results which followed the use of the supposedly innocent Ouija Board came to my notice and my observations led me into research in psychic phenomena for a possible explanation of these strange occurrences.[4]

Pastor H. Richard Neff notes that the Ouija board and other occult devices primarily work through autosuggestion. Yet he concludes:

A sufficient number of people have got into serious psychological difficulty through the use of a Ouija board to warn us that these instruments may not be "innocent toys." Most serious students of parapsychology strongly advise people not to use Ouija boards and such instruments.[5]

Hugh Lynn Cayce states:

We probably see and hear from more of those who are in trouble than most organizations of this kind. All of the psychiatrists I have talked with about this mention a few cases of disturbance that have resulted from Ouija boards and automatic writing.[6]

In his chapter "Automatic Writing and Ouija Boards" in _Venture Inward_, Cayce presents several case histories from his files. He introduces the topic by noting, "The frightening thing about them is that they can be duplicated by the thousands from the case histories of present-day inmates of mental institutions all over the world."[7]

Sometimes users who ignore such warnings later admonish others not to become involved with the Ouija board or similar methods of occult communication. One woman wrote: "Please warn others that the Ouija board and automatic writing are dangerous."[8] Another woman tried a variety of means to communicate with the supernatural, including the Ouija board, but she achieved success with automatic writing. She related how the spirit tormented her and even suggested suicide. She urged Cayce to warn others: "Can you also get some books on the market telling people of the danger of playing at these psychic things? I'm sure that I'm not the only foolish person who tries these things."[9]

The following account describes yet another unsuspecting Ouija participant who learned not to dabble in the occult. In January 1975 Coralee Leon, the editor of *House and Garden* magazine, attended a party with twenty other professionals whom she had never met. As the party progressed, the guests began to share various psychic and occult experiences. Arnold Copper, an interior and architectural designer, explained how his own skepticism of the occult underwent a radical change following the summer of 1967, which he spent with three friends on Fire Island, New York. One evening at their beach house, Copper and his friends fashioned a Ouija board and successfully contacted the spirit world, the first of fourteen seance sessions over a six-week period. An entity named Zelda told them about her life, which ended with her drowning in a shipwreck in 1873. Other spirit contacts included evil Bethelene and Higgins. When Zelda was in control, the glass moved smoothly over the table, but when Bethelene took over, the movement was violent. Typical Ouija manifestations occurred—the board spelled out profanities, the room temperature plummeted, apparitions materialized, one participant experienced a temporary possession, and fuzzy shapes mysteriously appeared in a Polaroid picture. Copper even had a near fatal car accident when the car seemed to wrench itself out of his control. On another occasion a "huge black chandelier began flashing on and off, on and off . . . tore loose from the ceiling and crashed down on the table, grazing" one of them. The seances ended with an apport (the sudden appearance of an object produced by a spiritualistic medium): "There in the center [of the coffee table] was a little pool of water, and in it lay a starfish, pulsating rhythmically."[10]

After hearing of Copper's experience, Leon urged him to consider publishing his story, and eventually they agreed to collaborate on such a book. At the beginning of _Psychic Summer_ Copper affirms: "The events described in this book are true. Some of the characters are well-known personalities whom many readers will recognize,"[11] so most names were changed. Leon concludes the book with a short postscript stating that she was able to verify some parts of the Ouija information during a stay in London.

The seances certainly altered the worldview of the four friends: "Certainly none of us had considered reincarnation or believed we would be born again. This experience opened our minds to the possibility of other states of existence. . . ."[12] Following the Fire Island experience Copper participated in two more seances. The first one had disastrous results—one person fainted and another became violently ill. In the last seance, Copper received information about his family history that was unknown to any of the operators of the board. Copper concludes: "The forces one deals with are of unknown power and proportions, and should be left utterly alone. I have never again attempted—nor will I ever—to contact the spirit world."[13]

In _The Guide Book for the Study of Psychical Research_, the glossary entry under "Ouija Board," notes:

> Many researchers have pointed out the inherent dangers of using the Ouija board or of taking its "messages" seriously, because of the possibility of dredging up some very unpleasant and potentially dis-

turbing attitudes and facts from one's subconscious. There have been numerous instances of persons who have become very upset emotionally from the use of the Ouija board.[14]

In *Confessions of a Psychic,* Susy Smith explains how her spirit communicators advised her.

Warn people away from Ouijas and automatic writing until you have learned how to be fully protected. They say that innocent efforts at communication are as dangerous as playing with matches or hand grenades. They have me as Exhibit A of what not to do, for I experienced many of the worst problems of such involvement. Had I been forewarned by my reading that such efforts might cause one to run the risk of being mentally disturbed, I might have been more wary. That is why my story is now being made public—just in the effort to prevent others from getting into situations which might prove more damaging to them than they fortunately did to me.[15]

Whether one accepts these spirit warnings or not, Miss Smith's own experiences warn against such involvements.

Manly P. Hall, lecturer and founder of the Philosophical Research Society, is considered to be one of the best-known authors and teachers on the occult in this century. Hall had numerous contacts with Ouija board users.

During the last twenty-five years [before 1944] I have had considerable personal experience with persons who have complicated their lives through dabbling with the Ouija board. Out of every hundred such cases, at least 95 are worse off for the experience. Some have suffered years of personal unhappiness as the penalty for the disorganization which this little table has brought into their lives. I know of broken homes, estranged families, and even suicides that can be traced directly to this source. In some cases health has suffered seriously and in others the psychic dabbling has led to serious financial losses. The remaining five out of every hundred actually secured information which was valuable or important to them. . . . Even in these cases, however, the Ouija board was not solutional in any general way. . . .

A number of persons who have used the Ouija board or other psychical devices have received messages purporting to come from divine or superhuman source. I have seen a number of messages variously attributed to Jesus, Buddha, Plato, and various angels and archangels. Such communication of course overwhelms the recipient, and works havoc with his ego.
. . .

I have examined a great number of these awful revelations; and while they may bear the authentic signature of some great person, the content always belies the signature. Yet perfectly honest persons, when convinced that they have been ordained by the spirit world to work in their time great earth solutions, develop evangelical zeal, and the result is disastrous in every sense of the word.[16]

Ed Warren, who spent years dealing with Ouija board cases, warns:

Ouija boards are just as dangerous as drugs. They're not to be played with. . . . Just as parents are responsible for other aspects of their children's lives, they should take equal care to keep the tools of the devil from their children . . . especially in an era when satanic cults are on the rise. Remember: Seances and Ouija boards and other occult paraphernalia are dangerous because evil spirits often disguise themselves as your loved ones—and take over your life.[17]

British Pastor Russell Parker, author of *Battling the Occult*, has counselled and advised many occult victims. Here are his comments on the Ouija board.

> I consider the Ouija board to be a dangerous occult door through which people have unwittingly opened themselves up to destructive powers. In so doing they have set themselves on a dangerous road which will only produce further spiritual deterioration.[18]

A number of writers caution that certain types of individuals should never engage in psychic experimentation or investigation. Dr. Hereward Carrington (1880–1958) was a leading psychical researcher and writer who did not accept biblical injunctions against occult experimentation. He was skeptical of occult phenomena, calling it psychopathic, and believed that participants would require treatment to restore their mental health. He felt that "the supposed 'dangers' connected with this subject lie almost wholly with the investigator and not with the subject matter investigated."[19] Dr. Carrington frequently advised those with unstable nervous and mental equilibrium to leave the occult alone. Unfortunately such people are most often attracted to the subject and "*are* in danger if they 'dabble in the occult.'"[20] Christians cannot accept Carrington's anti-biblical bias or his interpretation of the supernatural, but they should not ignore his warnings about the possible psychological problems that result from occult investigation.

Dr. Harmon H. Bro, a social scientist, a specialist in depth psychology, and director of the Bro Clinic did not discourage psychic development, although he offered some sensible suggestions. Bro believed that *motivation* was the most basic prerequisite for a common sense approach to psychic development. He explained that "psychologists use the term 'set' to encompass briefly the motives, attitudes, intents or purpose with which a person enters a particular experience, as a shortening for 'the set of one's mind and drives.'"[21] Bro then expanded on the problems the wrong "set" may create in psychic experimentation. His own files indicate that the cultivation of psychic ability is not to be taken lightly.

> Untold numbers of individuals undertake cultivation of psychic ability with a set toward personal or professional notoriety, toward gambling advantage or toward sexual conquest—and appear to achieve paranormal phenomena with few ill effects. But far more persons who try the same procedures for these same reasons embark on a course of increasingly distraught behavior, compulsive actions, alienation from friends and relatives and finally multiple-personality symptoms or suicide. To seek psychic ability without attention to one's set, then, is to play psychological Russian Roulette—like being hypnotized by a stranger of unknown training and intent.
>
> Even those who should be psychologically sophisticated are vulnerable where set is concerned, for some of the dominant motives in one's set may be hidden from consciousness. . . .
>
> The proportion of casualties because of set among those in the modern West who seek to cultivate psychic ability is probably quite large. A quick review of 22 cases in my own files where I personally have observed individuals training psychic capacity for four months to 20 years shows that about half of the cases achieved positive results with favorable consequences for their careers and health. The other half show mental and physical illness, divorce, vocational calamity, drug addiction and sexual deviation.[22]

If Bro's statement that "some of the dominant motives in one's set may be hidden from consciousness" is true, then the possibility exists that anyone who attempts to cultivate psychic ability could experience difficulties. From the biblical viewpoint, no one can really know himself or herself sufficiently well to be on safe ground: "The heart is more deceitful than all else and is desperately sick; who can understand it" (Jer. 17:9).

Dr. Thelma Moss, a certified psychologist on the staff of UCLA's Neuropsychiatric Institute and a researcher in parapsychology, prefaced her discussion on the Ouija board in this way: "Warning! For certain persons, the Ouija board is *no game* and can cause serious dissociations of personality."[23] She illustrates her warning with an actual case from the correspondence of a woman "who claimed to have developed automatic writing after practicing the Ouija board"—a normal progression. About a year later, the woman and her husband met Dr. Moss. She then requested to see the doctor in private.

> As soon as we were alone, the woman, with a look of triumph, told me that her "guide" had a message for me. Whereupon the woman promptly closed her eyes, reopened them, and announced that she was now the Virgin Mary and that the woman through whom she was speaking was going to follow in her footsteps. . . . Her automatic writing had helped to begin the split in her personality, which led to the schizophrenia for which she was hospitalized.[24]

A booklet published by the Evangelical Alliance of England quotes a number of psychiatric professionals who urge people not to use the Ouija board or other devices.

> Consultant psychiatrist Dr. Stuart Checkley [dean of the Institute of Psychiatry, Maudsley Hospital, London] says, "I have seen patients whose involvement with relatively minor forms of the occult has caused them to suffer mental illness. I have seen someone who as a result of one experiment with a Ouija board suffered frightening experiences outside his control, including automatic hand writing. He found himself writing frightening messages to himself."

Concludes Dr. Checkley, "Such things as Ouija boards and tarot cards can definitely harm. They open up the mind to outside forces. . . ."

Consultant child psychiatrist Dr. Graham Melville Thomas has encountered cases where children have been damaged as a result of the occult. Involvement such as Ouija boards are, he says, "potentially damaging and can unbalance children who are vulnerable."[25]

The Danger of Possession

Hans Holzer and other researchers in the occult do not discourage psychic investigation for those who are well prepared, but they do admit that the danger of possession exists.

> Those who wish to use the Ouija board as a parlor game I advise to think twice. There is always the possibility—rare, I admit, but conceivable—that one of those playing the board is a genuine trance medium without realizing it.
>
> In such a case, the board can become an easy entrance for a disincarnate person [the Christian would say demon] who might next take over the personality of the medium and manifest under conditions where no controls are possible. This is even more dangerous when dealing with table tipping.[26]

Rev. Horace Westwood notes that Dr. Elwood Worcester in his book _Body, Mind and Spirit_ presents actual case histories where the user's personality was invaded by outside entities. Westwood then concludes,

> Regardless of the truth of his contention, I could not help being struck by his observation that nearly all the cases he described had developed as a conse-

quence of tampering with psychic matters, either in the form of "Ouija" or of automatic writing.[27]

Rev. Donald Page of the Christian Spiritualist Church practices exorcism. He found that "the majority of possession cases . . . are people who have used the Ouija board."[28] Youth worker Gary Wilburn spent over two years researching his book on the occult, *The Fortune Sellers*. He warns:

> The ease with which a Ouija board can be procured, coupled with an inherent fascination to the novice, makes it one of the most deadly of all spiritualist "devices." The operator of a Ouija board is easy prey for evil spirits.[29]

And finally, this account explains how one skeptical professional became a believer in the occult.

> Psychiatrist Dr. Michael David admits to having been "extremely dubious" about possession and occult activity. But he now takes "a very different view." Called to help a 15-year-old anorexic while attending a Christian holiday, he found the frail teenager having a fit and virtually holding clear of the ground the four adults attempting to restrain her, "She was coming out with incredible mouthfuls of obscenity and abuse," he recalls. "It quickly became obvious that her problem was not anorexia, but severe demonic possession. It later emerged that she had been involved with Ouija boards and her brother with black magic."[30]

Ouija Users Dilute or Deny Christianity

Both Christian and non-Christian writers acknowledge that any communication from the "other side" (whether through mediums, channeling, automatic writing, a pendulum, the

Ouija board, or other means) denies the essential doctrines of the Christian faith. William O. Stevens cites a number of "spirit" messages that were recorded by people from a "wide variety of backgrounds, from High Churchman to agnostic."[31] In these communications,

> orthodox theology has no place, in spite of the fact that all who received them have been brought up in that tradition. . . .
>
> At any rate, in these communications many dogmas of the Christian churches are passed over in tacit denial if not specifically contradicted. There is no reference to Original Sin, the Trinity, the Resurrection of the Body, Judgment Day, the importance of baptism, absolution, the Vicarious Atonement, and so on.[32]

A woman in England (we'll call her Ann) began using a homemade Ouija board in her early teens and later became involved with other occult practices such as fortune-telling, palmistry, cartomancy, astrology, tarot cards, and crystal balls.[33] Ann eagerly read occult books and participated in hundreds of seances on her homemade board, directing questions to the "Spirit of the glass." Over 90 percent of the time she received a jumble of letters that would be repeated, letter for letter, over and over again. She came to the conclusion that these were either foreign or demonic names. Sometimes if she pressured the spirit contact she would get cooperation, and once she experienced a temperature drop and a terrifying presence. Later she used the manufactured board but without much success. Although Ann's experience was basically free of the more sensational psychic phenomena, for the twenty-five years she was involved in occult activities, she was unable to understand the Bible, even though she joined a church in her early teens. She stopped going to church and struggled for several years before returning. At this point Ann became a Christian and as a result began to have nightmares every night for a number of weeks. She was too frightened to tell anyone. The nightmares stopped after her baptism, but then a week later she had another dream.

> Suddenly I was seized from behind by horrible, grey tentacles—around my neck, waist, arms and legs, pulling me back. I knew who was behind me, so I couldn't say "Get thee behind me, Satan!" It was the worst moment of my life. I screamed out, "Dear Lord Jesus, save me!" Suddenly, at the end of the passage ahead of me appeared the brilliant white light I had seen in my [earlier] desert dreams. The tentacles slithered away and then I woke up, drenched with perspiration. I had had enough. I had to see my minister. When I related to him the foregoing dreams, he said at once, "You've been dabbling in the occult, haven't you?"
>
> "But it's only fun," I said, amazed that that should've been the first thing he'd mentioned, rather than that I might have been overdoing things.
>
> "Fun nothing," he snapped, and he opened his Bible to Deuteronomy 18:9–14. He made me read the verses out loud. When I came to the part where it said such practitioners were an "abomination to the LORD," I was stricken to the core of my being.

Ann systematically disposed of her occult materials and renounced her involvement. Every time she gave up some occult object, she felt better. Her occult involvement had prevented her from becoming a Christian for many years, and she had misled many other people in her life. She explained in her letter to me, "I am just glad to help; after all the harm I did in the past, it is good to be able to do this. I feel that I am redressing the balance, even in a small way."

The story of Rev. Stainton Moses (1839–92), a well-known medium and one of the earliest practitioners of automatic writing, is a perfect example of occult involvement resulting in a departure from orthodox Christianity. At first, Moses was "distressed and angered" by the doctrinal denials of the messages he received, but eventually he came to accept them. The following excerpt comes from his best-known work, _Spirit Teachings_ (often called the Bible of spiritualism).

> You will learn hereafter that the revelation of God is progressive, bounded by no time, confined to no people. . . . You will learn also that all revelation is made through a human channel; and consequently cannot but be tinctured in some measure with human error. No revelation is plenary inspiration. . . . Weigh what is said. If it be commended by reason, receive it; if not, reject it. . . . The inspiration is divine, but the medium is human. . . . To imagine that an opinion uttered many centuries ago is of binding force eternally is mere folly.[34]

William Stevens adds, "More than one communicator stresses the need of new revelation, and points out the fact that 'there is no monopoly of truth in any religion.'"[35] Spirit communications both stress the need for new revelation and deny the truth of the Bible. Christians believe the Bible to be God's _only_ revelation to guide and direct us. According to the Westminster Shorter Catechism, Question 2: "The Word of God, which is contained in the Scriptures of the Old and New Testaments, is the only rule to direct us how we may glorify and enjoy him." Christians believe that no further _revelation_ is needed. Clearly the spirits who claim to reveal new revelation contradict Scripture's own claim to be the only infallible guide to belief and practice.

John Weldon is a co-author of several recently published books on the occult. He summarizes his findings by saying: "The personal research of the author into scores of spirit-written books brings out one common fact; they all deny basic Christian doctrines. Some are more subtle than others, but _there are no exceptions_ he can find."[36]

From his investigations into the occult, Catholic writer J. Godfrey Raupert provides the following enlightening observations:

> When trust and confidence have been secured, the spirit will slowly begin to undermine any true Christian foundation that may exist, deny the divinity of Christ, the authority of conscience, the responsibility of human life, and the reality of a judgment to come. It will feed the mind on empty platitudes, very acceptable to the natural man, but ultimately contradictory of the very fundamental truths of the Christian religion. The very circumstance, known to all the world, that those who embrace Spiritism always cease to profess historic Christianity in any form is in itself ample proof in support of this statement.[37]

What about more complex or progressive attempts to contact the supernatural by those "who scorn the trivialities of the seance but try to discover from the advanced spirits a philosophy of the universe"?[38] J. Stafford Wright agrees with other Christian writers when he observes:

> Without any exception that I have discovered, these communicators deny the deity of Jesus Christ (except in the nonbiblical sense that we are all allegedly sons of God) and His atoning death. These are the unique facts of revealed Christianity; and if they are abandoned, Christianity becomes just one of the several religions of the world.[39]

One of my own students became involved with the Ouija board.[40] One evening he and three friends from church decided to hold a seance. They set up the board, lit some candles, darkened the room, and began to call on the spirits by asking: "May we have Satan in our presence." The pointer started to spin in circles and flew off the table. After replacing the pointer, they asked if Satan were present and the indicator moved to YES. All four became frightened when the answers were too accurate for mere coincidence. The candles dimmed and a feeling of evil pervaded the room. One boy threw his New Testament on the Ouija board, but it scooted off in a different direction. The boys prayed for the evil presence to leave the room, but it seemed to remain with them. On the way home, the boys felt the evil so intently that they stopped the car and prayed on the front lawn of a neighborhood church. This experience ended their use of the Ouija board, but the effects of the incident continued.

Shortly after this incident, all four young men began to doubt their Christian faith; three stopped attending church. After several weeks two seemed to develop different personalities and one of them experienced serious problems of oppression. Another became strongly opposed to Christianity and would argue with his friend at every opportunity. At this point, my student came to me for advice. I urged him to renounce his use of the board, destroy it, and ask God to deliver all four from the occult power of this experience. On his way home to carry out the instructions, the student seemed to hear a voice warning him not to destroy the board. After breaking the board and burning it, he became violently nauseated. But disposing of the board brought a renewed sense of victory in his Christian life.

The Sunday after he destroyed the board, the student was surprised to find his antagonistic friend in church. He asked him why he was there and his friend replied, "I don't know; I just started thinking about going to church on Friday." Friday was the day the student destroyed the Ouija board.

Dr. Kenneth McAll was a missionary-surgeon in China during World War II. After the war he returned to England and studied psychiatry in London and Edinburgh. For a number of years he practiced as a consultant psychiatrist in the United States and England. In an article published in 1975, he notes that he had worked with "280 cases involving exorcism." In the ten cases summarized in the article, he refers to the connection that people involved in the occult feel, even when they are no longer in the same physical location. When the occult control is broken for one participant through prayer, renunciation, or exorcism (or any combination of these), a healing or release may occur for another person(s) many miles away.[41]

Conclusion

The Ouija experiences in this chapter are fairly typical. Many users conclude that the board works because its predictions are successful, its information is accurate, they experience a good or evil presence, room temperature drops, they find lost items, or the planchette flies off the board. Various physical manifestations, apparitions, apports, and attempted or actual possession demonstrate something extraordinary is occurring. Although the game's messages are initially benign and friendly, they may deteriorate to the vile, vulgar, suggestive, and even threatening. Other users develop further occult interest in direct voice mediumship, automatic writing, and Ouija or occult addiction.

Gina Covina's observations in *The Ouija Book* are typical of other published accounts with a spiritualist worldview.[42] Her explanation of "Absolute Truth" is consistent with other Ouija reports and represents a denial of the biblical worldview: "The voices are emphatic and unanimous in their insistence that we *are* God."[43] "The idea that evil is simply the nondevelopment of good . . . echoes through every deeply pursued Ouija experience I've encountered."[44] "Love *is* God. Love *is* the universe, as God or consciousness is the universe."[45] "Ouija is a tool through which we become more and more conscious that we are God. Let's say it in the bluntest way possible: the Ouija board is a tool through which we become God."[46]

Sometimes when users question the board to reveal the source of its messages, the pointer spells out "Satan" or a demonic equivalent. Bruce Larson notes:

I've talked with hundreds of people who have played with Ouija. Without exception, those who have asked the board to disclose its source of information have received the response: "demons, devils, Satan, Beelzebub, Lucifer," or a satanic equivalent. Either unconscious assumptions were made by the players, triggering muscular responses, to the question, or the reply was truthful. If the latter, the Ouija board is a spiritually dangerous tool of evil invasion.[47]

For some Christians, Ouija use results in spiritual lethargy and decline, but renunciation of the board leads to ultimate deliverance. For skeptics, the Ouija experience may produce a belief in the supernatural, but it is usually in the area of reincarnation. A number of the Ouija board users discountinue using it, sometimes warning others against it and vowing never to use it again themselves.

When people use the Ouija board for occult purposes, it often indicates their dissatisfaction with rationalism and materialism and a desire for a vital supernatural experience. The Bible teaches that there are only two personally defined sources of supernatural power and guidance: God and Satan. Occult involvement seeks to find spiritual reality outside of God and his revelation. It represents an erroneous approach to the ultimate meaning of human existence.

Notes

1. Raymond Bayless and William Addams Welch, "Ouija Boards: Dangerous Toys? or Useful Psychic Tools," _Probe the Unknown_ (July 1975): 25–26.
2. Ibid., 55.
3. Ibid., 25.
4. Carl A. Wickland, _Thirty Years Among the Dead,_ 2d ed. (National Psychological Institute, 1924), 16–17.
5. H. Richard Neff, _Psychic Phenomena and Religion_ (Philadelphia: Westminster Press, 1971), 131.
6. Hugh Lynn Cayce, letter to the author, May 4, 1972.
7. Hugh Lynn Cayce, _Venture Inward_ (New York: Paperback Library, 1964), 130.

8. Harold Sherman, *Your Mysterious Powers of ESP* (New York: World, 1969), 126–27.

9. Letter in the A.R.E. files, Virginia Beach, Virginia.

10. Arnold Copper and Coralee Leon, *Psychic Summer: A True Account of a Menacing Experience on Fire Island* (New York: Dial, 1976), 179.

11. Ibid., author's statement.

12. Ibid., 182.

13. Ibid. 182–83.

14. Robert H. Ashby, *The Guide Book for the Study of Psychical Research* (New York: Weiser, 1972), 182.

15. Susy Smith, *Confessions of a Psychic* (New York: Macmillan, 1971), 75.

16. Manly P. Hall, "The Devil's Flatiron," *Horizon* (Oct.-Dec. 1944): 76–77.

17. Ed and Lorraine Warren with David Chase, *Graveyard* (New York: St. Martin's, 1992), 137–38.

18. Russell Parker, letter to the author, Nov. 8, 1992.

19. Hereward Carrington, "Is It Wrong to Study Psychic Phenomena?" *Fate* (Nov.-Dec. 1961): 71.

20. Ibid., 66–67.

21. Harmon H. Bro, "Are There Dangers in Psychic Development?" *Fate* (Feb. 1971): 102.

22. Ibid., 102–3.

23. Thelma Moss, *The Probability of the Impossible* (Los Angeles: Tarcher, 1974), 237.

24. Ibid., 239–40.

25. *Doorways to Danger* (London: Evangelical Alliance, 1987), 2–3.

26. Hans Holzer, *ESP and You* (New York: Hawthorn, 1966), 74–75.

27. Horace Westwood, *There Is a Psychic World* (New York: Crown, 1949), 189.

28. Francoise Strachan, "A Company of Devils," *Man, Myth and Magic* (number 73): after 2060.

29. Gary Wilburn, *The Fortune Sellers* (Glendale: Gospel Light, 1972), 195.

30. *Doorways to Danger*, 3.

31. William O. Stevens, *Psychics and Common Sense* (New York: Dutton, 1953), 230.

32. Ibid., 238.

33. The following summary comes from E. J. A., written testimony and letter to the author, May 12, 1992.

34. Stevens, *Psychics*, 239.

35. Ibid.

36. John Weldon, *The Consequences of Psychic Involvement: A Look at Some Hazards* (manuscript), 260.

37. J. Godfrey Raupert, "The Truth About the Ouija Board," *Ecclesiastical Review* (Nov. 1918): 472.

38. J. Stafford Wright, *Christianity and the Occult* (Chicago: Moody, 1971), 115.
39. Ibid.
40. The following account comes from an interview with the author, Sept. 1969.
41. Kenneth McAll, "The Ministry of Deliverance," *Expository Times* (July 1975): 296–98.
42. Gina Covina, *The Ouija Book* (New York: Simon and Schuster, 1979), 138–51.
43. Ibid., 144.
44. Ibid., 146.
45. Ibid., 147.
46. Ibid., 153.
47. Bruce Larson, *Satanism: The Seduction of America's Youth* (Nashville: Nelson, 1989), 56–57.

6

The Ouija's Popularity with Children and Teenagers

In his book *Occult America*, John Godwin defined a new trend in the Ouija board revival that began in the mid-1960s. Adult users of the board "were joined by millions of teenagers, right down to the thirteen-year-old level, who had never previously shown much interest in these gadgets."[1] From my own study of hundreds of accounts, I believe that Ouija experimentation begins much earlier—with children aged six or even younger. One user wrote, "When I was very small my mother bought an Ouija board, and we played with it on rainy days."[2] Parker Brothers itself recommends the board for ages eight to adult.

Children and teenagers learn about the board from numerous sources—television, movies, music, and books. Although many of them only use the board casually, some become seriously dependent on it, and therefore it is essential that parents be made aware of the Ouija board's dangers.

The Ouija Board and Children

Children are exposed to the Ouija board at a very early age through books, television, films, and even in school.

Children's Books. *Teddy Ruxpin* is a book and audio series for children. In one adventure, *The Missing Princess,* Teddy and his friends visit the Wizard of Wee Gee. One illustration shows Teddy, his friends, and the Wizard all seated around a Ouija-like instrument that has alphabet characters in a circle with a pointer. They watch to see what was being spelled. On the cassette we hear,

> [Teddy] "But we were very impressed by the Wizard. We all sat down at a big table."
>
> [Wizard] "Now everyone concentrate, so that we can bring forth the mystical powers of communication. . . . I said concentrate! I think we are making contact. Everyone concentrate on where Princess Aruzia could be."
>
> [Teddy] "The pointer on the Wizard's table began moving. It slid around, pointing at first to one letter and then another. It would spell out "G-U-T-A-N-G-S. Gutangs."[3]

Many children's books and comics communicate an occult theme, but some specifically target the Ouija experiences of their fictional characters. For example in *How a Weirdo and a Ghost Can Change Your Entire Life,* the summary states: "Martha braves class ridicule to befriend a 'weirdo,' who enriches her life with his Ouija board and proves to be a better friend than those she lost."[4] Award-winning author Patricia Windsor presents an accurate account of Ouija experimentation. In the story Martha and her "weirdo" friend Teddy (apparently a nine- or ten-year-old) never treat the Ouija as a "game," but as a way to contact the dead and to gain other information. The book accurately describes the board—Martha even checks the dictionary for the words "Ouija" and "planchette."

Teddy explains, "'You get the best results when it's dark.'" "'Now,' he said, 'Who do you know who's dead?'" Teddy "put his fingers on the planchette and told Martha to concentrate. . . . 'Make your mind go blank.'"[5] They fail on their initial attempt, and Martha puts the board under her bed. Later she tries it alone, and when she asks for "Uncle Archie," the board begins to work. The word that is spelled out proves to have evidential value. Martha then reasons, "If it was so easy to summon someone from the spirit world," why not ask for other information?[6] When Teddy learns about what happened, he warns her that instead of contacting "the person you ask for," sometimes "other spirits just barge in and give messages. Some of them can be a little unfriendly."[7] Teddy also suggests that Martha might be a "medium," and recommends that she keep a scientific notebook of the messages.

Again Martha works the board alone and contacts "Uncle Archie." Typical Ouija board phenomena occur, such as the rapid and energetic movement of the planchette, the drop in room temperature, the intrusion of another spirit ("Pinky"), and a wind that sweeps through the room knocking over small items. Martha is frightened. "Ghosts could sure get mad. She would remember to stay on their good side from now on."[8] At the school library she asks for books on ghosts. Teddy and Martha are invited to attend Diane's Halloween party, and she tells them that she is having a difficult time thinking of things to do at the party.

> "I could make a suggestion," Teddy said. "But it could get pretty spooky."
> "The spookier the better!" Diane said. "What is it?"
> Teddy gave Martha a look. "A surprise," he said. "What do you think, Martha? Halloween is a good time for ghosts. Should we help out?"
> Martha smiled. "Sure," she said.[9]

This children's book provides an accurate account of Ouija mediumship and could lead young readers to believe that Ouija board seances are exciting though scary.

Terry Ann Modica recounts her own Ouija board use and entrapment in *The Power of the Occult*. "I was almost a teenager. I assumed the Ouija board was just a game. I believed what I'd heard; that it worked by releasing hidden answers from my subconscious mind."[10] She began to read occult books, then learned hypnosis and even conducted seances. She became so obsessed with the occult that for a while she turned away from her Christian faith.[11] Later Modica wrote a teen novel, *The Dark Secret of the Ouija,*[12] which accurately describes Ouija board use and presents deliverance from a Christian perspective.

School Usage. Through correspondence, interviews, or from published accounts, I have discovered that the Ouija board is sometimes used in school by students or made available by a teacher. This usually occurs with teenagers, but I have heard of cases where the board is used in elementary classes. In 1987

> a sixth-grade teacher in Southern California [Ontario-Montclair School District] made the headlines of his local paper when he refused to remove a Ouija board from his classroom. He saw nothing wrong with the game and felt his First Amendment rights were at stake. Concerned parents went to the school board calling for the game's removal.[13]

The school board held a series of public hearings on the Ouija topic from April 6–29, 1987, and accepted written statements through May 4. The committee issued its report on June 15.[14] In spite of massive documentation on the occult nature of the Ouija board, the report concluded, "Based on the facts that the materials are not verified by empirical research data and that there is ambiguity, subjectivity, and a wide variance of personal opinion within the material, the Committee does not make a judgment on this issue."[15]

The *High Action Reading for Study Skills* by Modern Curriculum Press (1979 ed.) "that were designed for third- to sixth-graders . . . featured eight pages on the Ouija board!" At one point the material suggests, "You might have fun making your own magic board and trying it out with a friend. There are many ways you can do it."[16] After explaining how to make a simple Ouija board, the material adds, "ask a question and wait to see what happens!"[17]

Near the end of her chapter on "Schools and Counterfeit Spirituality," Berit Kjos concludes:

> An increasing number of schools are telling students to research the occult, to role-play occult fantasy games such as Dungeons and Dragons, and to seek esoteric knowledge through horoscopes, I Ching, and Ouija boards. Needless to say, the children are playing with an incredible fire that neither they nor their teachers can control.[18]

Television. Television is another way children are exposed to the Ouija board through a noncritical medium. During October 1992, I noticed two evening programs that included the board. One of them, "Camp Wilder," depicted the Ouija in a typical game fashion—"Hey, a Ouija board, let's play." Parker Brothers commercials for the Ouija board sometimes appear during Saturday morning cartoons.

Mediumistic Psychosis. Stoker Hunt presents two cases involving children in what Professor Hans Bender identifies as "mediumistic psychosis."[19] The first incident concerns an almost twelve-year-old girl who played the Ouija board with her friends. The board predicted she would die at the age of thirteen. Her parents did not pay much attention to this prediction until they realized the impact it had on their daughter. The mother writes:

> We eventually couldn't ignore the changes in her life, i.e., avoiding going out very far from home, dreading

trips, taking illness like the common cold very seriously. Our daughter was very fearful, often speaking of her dread and crying many times. The tension was building in our family and we found *ourselves* becoming frightened for her *and* us, because she believed it so much. . . . We weren't sure what was happening, but on the day of her thirteenth birthday, she boldly announced that she had fooled the Ouija game![20]

The second case concerns

a happy, gregarious 11-year-old who suddenly turned into a terrified little child, afraid to leave her home, convinced she was about to be struck dead—all because of one particular session with the Ouija board. The quality of her schoolwork dropped from excellent to failing. She lost weight. She developed symptoms of paranoia.[21]

She was cured after a number of sessions with a psychiatrist.

The Ouija Board and Teenagers

Research and published accounts establish that a large number of teenagers have "played" with the Ouija board, although there are presently no statistics available on the extent of such use. Neil Anderson (a seminary professor) and Steve Russo (a youth evangelist) developed a survey to determine the occult exposure of 286 students in a Christian high school. The "startling responses" to their survey prompted them to broaden their research. "We surveyed 1725 students (433 junior high and 1292 senior high) attending Christian schools and camps. . . . Question 9 asked students to indicate if they had participated in certain occultic practices."[22]

The survey questioned students about a variety of occult practices—astral projection, table-lifting, fortunetelling, astrology, Dungeons and Dragons, crystals or pyramids, automatic writing, tarot cards, palm reading, spirit guides, blood pacts, and the Ouija board. Fifteen percent of the junior high students surveyed claimed to have used the Ouija board; for senior high students the percentage was even higher—26 percent. Ouija board use ranked second to Dungeons and Dragons (18 percent to 15 percent) for junior high students, but first for those in senior high, followed by astrology (20 percent) and Dungeons and Dragons (16 percent). When the figures from junior and senior high are combined, the Ouija board becomes the leading device in this sampling. Later the authors state, "It is disconcerting that 416 of the Christian kids we surveyed [out of 1725] had been involved with Ouija boards at some time."[23]

Randy Emon, a California police sergeant, is listed in the *Occult Crime: A Law Enforcement Primer*[24] as a law enforcement officer with expertise in occult-related crime investigations and as a contributor to the *Primer*.[25] After speaking with Officer Emon, I asked him to summarize his work and findings.

Since 1985, I began researching and investigating occult-related crimes, subsequently developing a slide presentation geared toward the public, law enforcement, the church, and educators. As a result, this presentation has been shown to an estimated audience of 20,000 attendees, of which about 25% were from law enforcement. Additionally in late 1986, I founded an organization called the Christian Occult Investigators Network (C.O.I.N.) which recently disbanded. As a result of the law enforcement classes coupled with C.O.I.N., I interviewed about 1500 teenagers between 1985 and 1992 who were involved with some aspect of occult involvement. Their activities ranged from participating in reading occult-type comic books, playing computer fantasy role-playing games, Dungeons and Dragons, tarot cards, reading witchcraft books and novels, reading books about satanism or actually participating in witchcraft or satanic rituals. About 75% or more of these participants were either currently living in a Christian family, had made a commitment to serve Jesus Christ, had a Christian up-bringing, or were currently attending a Catholic or Protestant church.

When attempting to pinpoint the reasons why they decided to partake in these activities, several common reasons arose. Many were introduced to these practices by their friends and were simply cu-rious to see some tangible results. They were some-what disenchanted with their family religion and felt the occult would offer some fast solutions.

Better than two-thirds interviewed said the main item of curiosity that caused them to continue a deeper interest in occult study was their experimentation with the Ouija board. About one-fifth said it was Dungeons and Dragons. Of the two-thirds that began using the Ouija board, better than fifty percent obtained addi-tional occult-type literature either from a library, from friends or from a local book store to further their stud-ies. Of the remaining fifty percent, about ninety per-cent made a conscious decision to abandon their ef-forts to continue seeking occult knowledge as none perceived *any* desired results. Of the latter group, al-most all who were Christians fell almost totally away from serving the Lord or reading the Bible.

Once these participants decided to abandon their efforts to dabble with occult practices, most returned to their Christian faith. Prior to returning to Chris-tianity, many developed symptoms as listed. . . . [See: Symptoms of Occult Activity Involvement, below.][26]

Of special significance is Emon's finding that "better than two-thirds interviewed said the main item of curiosity that caused them to continue a deeper interest in occult study was their experimentation with the Ouija board," and that of these over "fifty percent obtained additional occult-type literature." Students who are raised in a Christian home or who professed faith in Christianity were not exempt from occult experimentation.

Emon lists the "Symptoms of Occult Activity Involvement Compiled from Actual Case Studies and Interviews as of September 1989." Certainly not all these symptoms would be present in any one individual, but Ouija board case studies and research indicate that a number of them are symptomatic of extensive Ouija use.

> Frightening, recurring nightmares
> Voices
> Insomnia
> Apparitions
> Suicidal/murderous thoughts
> Attempted suicide
> Extremely secretive demeanor
> Time loss/memory gap
> Violent behavior
> Poltergeist activity
> Depression/withdrawal from society
> Drug use
> Physical contact by a seen or unseen entity, sometimes sexual
> Involuntary muscle spasm—not associated with drug use. Also described as a shaking or vibrating bed or the sensation of mild earthquakes.
> Change in clothing style (not in all cases)
> Change in behavior
> Obsession with fantasy role playing games such as Dungeons and Dragons
> Obsession with occult-related novels and related books
> Electrical sensation in the body from mild to very sharp
> Atmospheric temperature changes

Feeling of leaving one's body (astral projection)
Possession of occult paraphernalia/books/games
Aversion to the Bible or Christian related material;
[symptoms] such as words blurring or similar to
dyslexia; or falling asleep when reading Scripture.[27]

Emon reported the following case of a troubled seven-teen-year-old boy whose Ouija board spirit contact invited the boy to join him in a more pleasant world. For a young person with personal problems, such an invitation can seem alluring. The following transcription comes from the boy's suicide note left on a tape recorder for his parents. Along with the tape, his parents found a display of satanic and witchcraft items, record albums by Suicidal Tendencies and Venom, and a Ouija board. The boy was scheduled to be returned to juvenile hall the next day, and he didn't want to go.

You better brace yourself because I have some weird stuff to tell you. Some of it you might not understand. . . . One of the main questions I needed answered that I never got to was, "For what purpose was the spirit of my Ouija board wanting me to kill myself?" The reason I wanted to ask this is because I developed an odd sort of relationship with the board and I got to the point where I didn't even have to touch the board to get it to work at all . . . . All I had to do was to ask it the questions and every time I got a logical, bril-liant answer. Sometimes I didn't even have to ask anything, still it would talk to me.

Mom, you ask me why I'm so unsociable lately? Well, if you had a friend like this, you wouldn't need any friends. But anyway, one night, the board started to tell how heaven and hell don't exist and the way you die, and where you die, determine the intensity of your life after. The worse the death, the better the life. The better the atmosphere of your death, the bet-ter the atmosphere of your next life. See how it works!

There are no books to read, no rules to follow, no battle between good and evil. Good is in the atmosphere of your death and the evil is in the gruesomeness of your death. So I figured if everything else the board said was right, then this has to be right.

So then it asked me if I wanted to be with him forever in a totally civilized world with no problems, with only the people that I wanted to talk to there—and I said "yes." And he told me to get to where he was I had to commit suicide in a pretty gruesome way; and it would have to be in the mountains or in the sea—so I chose the mountains. And if you're wondering why your guns are missing Dad, I'm really sorry, but it's the only thing I can think of that was fast, and pretty gross, too. . . . I know I'll be happy and maybe I'll see you in about forty years or so.

. . . But if you ever want to talk to me, and you might think this is weird, too, but you can always use the Ouija board here and I'll probably be able to talk to you—anyway that's what the board said—that you might think I'm weird believing in what the board says, but everything it said so far is right. . . .[28]

Eight months later, the boy was located in another state. By that time, he had turned eighteen and his parents did not bring him home. Although in this case, the boy failed to commit suicide, Martin Ebon notes, "The cases are mounting up where men or women follow such 'messages' with slave-like obedience. . . . They may . . . even be invited by the communicating 'entity' to commit suicide to share its life after death."[29]

Contemporary Music. Even a cursory survey of the lyrics in contemporary rock music reveals the prominence of the occult message. "Album covers include such things as illustrations of devils' heads, crucified figures, demonic babies, skeletons, pentagrams, black candles and the occult number

666."[30] Al Menconi, an expert on contemporary music, reminds us that "music does affect listeners. Young people constantly look for answers to their most important questions." According to Menconi,

> a recent poll of 2,000 students in grades 7–12 showed that 68 percent of them regarded an entertainer as a hero. It's human nature to imitate our heros. When young people find someone who is attractive and interesting, they often begin to model themselves after that person.[31]

One such entertainer is Morrissey, the former lead singer for The Smiths. His popularity was demonstrated by the enthusiastic response to his 1991 U.S. debut tour and his recent return appearance in 1992. Reporting on his Hollywood Bowl engagement, music reviewer Chris Willman writes that "Morrissey is the perfect hero for that youthful contingent looking for someone to worship and to identify with at the same time."[32] What does all this have to do with the Ouija board?

Morrissey was featured under the headline, "Devil of a Row Over Hit."

> Pop star Morrissey was last night slammed for encouraging kids to toy with the Devil. His smash hit single "Ouija Board, Ouija Board" tells how he tried to contact a dead friend by using the occult game.
>
> Last night Diane Core, founder of the action group Childwatch, said: "This was an incredibly irresponsible thing to do. How anyone can be stupid enough to dabble with the spirit world is beyond me."
>
> But millionaire Morrissey . . . insisted the song was an attempt to "inject a higher standard of intelligence" into pop music.[33]

His song, "Ouija Board, Ouija Board" is in keeping with his previously expressed philosophy of life.

Ouija board would you work for me?
I have got to say Hello to an old friend
Ouija board, Ouija board would you work for me?
I have got to get through to a good friend
She has now gone from this Unhappy Planet
with all the carnivores and the destructors on it
Ouija board, Ouija board would you help me
Because I still feel so horribly lonely
would you, Ouija board would you, Ouija board
would you help me because I just can't find
my place in this world. . . .
The table is rumbling . . . the table is rumbling
the glass is moving. . . .[34]

Satanism and Satanic Recruitment. Is there any connection between the Ouija board and satanism? In his booklet *Teen Satanism: Redeeming the Devil's Children,* ex-occultist Greg Reid writes:

> The primary target for adult satanists right now is the youth. . . . In the last few years I have had a wide exposure to and involvement with teen satanists. Based on everything I've learned, the following presents a typical recruitment of a prospective teen satanist.[35]

After discussing the way in which the recruit is selected, he explains:

> Once the potential recruit takes the bait, this is what usually happens: . . . The recruit is invited to a party with a lot of other kids. Even though the leader is actually under another adult, other teens in his coven will not know this.
>
> There are lots of drugs, alcohol and sex with anyone you want. Female members offer themselves freely. After a while, Ouija boards and other occult games are brought in and played.

The potential recruit who shows an unusual interest with the occult games is approached by the leader.[36]

Because Reid noticed the prominence of the Ouija board and other occult games in the satanic recruitment process, I wrote him for more information. How did he reach his conclusions? What was his evidence? Reid answered:

The information contained in *Teen Satanism* concerning the use of Ouija boards to recruit teens is gleaned from interviews with over 100 teens over the past seven years, many of whom told me personally that this was their introduction into the occult world by someone who later turned them to satanism. In one instance, party fliers were put on cars at teen hangouts here in El Paso, and the host was a satanist recruiter who used D & D, Ouija and other occult games to introduce those who came to the party to the occult and later pulled them in deeper. Even now, many satanists STILL use Ouija boards, as they do most occult tools.[37]

Maureen Davies of Reachout Trust in Britain researches ritual abuse and works with its victims. She confirms that satanists have "organized parties where the Ouija board is introduced or tarot cards. . . . Gradually they are introduced to a third person who will tell them that Satan has the power."[38]

Sean Sellers murdered a convenience store clerk, his mother, and his stepfather at the age of sixteen as a result of his satanic activity. He writes of his own experience:

When I was a satanist the Ouija was used frequently as a way to introduce individuals into the occult. We knew the Ouija was accepted by most people as being harmless, and once we got a person playing, it was only a matter of time before they would agree to join us in a satanic ritual.[39]

Vicar George Mather worked at the Massachusetts State Correctional Institution in Bridgewater where he "met several inmates in the criminally insane section who apparently had led normal, productive lives until they started using the Ouija board. . . . An ex-satanist admitted his involvement started out with a Ouija board. He claimed to have always had a curiosity for things taboo. Curiosity turned into fascination."[40] The article does not give the age of the inmate when he began using the board or when he became a satanist, but the connection between satanism and the Ouija certainly existed in his case.

Some satanists use the Ouija board for divination, according to Johanna Michaelsen.

> I have spoken with those who have had close personal associations with satanism who tell me that some satanists do indeed use the Ouija board for the purpose of divination. Several police officers have confirmed this fact to me. At least one self-styled satanist youth gang in Southern California used the Ouija board to select the name of the gang's next victim from a list of people whom they consider to be "the most vulnerable to their mind control."[41]

One of my students wrote the following response to my questionnaire on the occult:

> The Ouija board has worked for me many times because I used to go to the meetings in San Francisco where Satan was worshiped, and one of the main ways of communicating with him and his demons was the Ouija board. I have not been in the same room with one since. I know the dangers.

In their discussion on the Ouija board, the authors of *The Seduction of Our Youth* write that "satanists have been known to crash Ouija board parties to help players learn how to 'really use the game.'"[42]

In addition to its connection with satanism, the Ouija board is also used to recruit teenagers into other occult practices, as one Christian author discovered in his conversation with a former warlock. "'I'd start with the Ouija board,' he told me. 'Kids thought that was fun. Then I'd encourage them in astrology.' He went on to elaborate the subtle ways in which young people are trapped before they realize it."[43]

Larry Jones, president of the Cult Crime Impact Network and editor of _File 18 Newsletter,_ stated that

> there have been a number of situations in the past seven years which have involved Ouija boards as one step in the downward spiral into occultism. It is a strong recruiting tool which piques interest in the occult. In many "deliverance" cases, use of the board (or a facsimile) seemed to be the entry point for demonic controls and harassment in the person's life. . . . In my opinion, it is more of a recruiting tool than the primary instrument of direction and control for seriously deviant behavior.[44]

Films. The Ouija board has been featured in several movie plots: _Deadly Messages_ aired on "ABC Thursday Night Movie" on February 21, 1985. _Witchboard_ came to theaters on March 13, 1987. _And You Thought Your Parents Were Weird_ appeared in 1991. And _Witchboard II: The Devil's Doorway_ appeared in 1993.

Deadly Messages was advertised in the newspaper television guide: "Is it a board game? Or can it tell the future? Is it a child's toy? Or a passage to the world of spirits? Now it's delivered a deadly message: I-AM-GOING-TO-KILL-YOU."[45] Both Cindy (who is later murdered) and Laura (who witnesses the murder) use the Ouija board in a typical seance fashion. "Is there anybody there?" "What's your name?" Linda becomes obsessed with the board and eventually is possessed. The film presents manifestations of an evil spirit that are typical of serious Ouija board use, such as the planchette moving without anyone's hands touching it, profanity, lowered room temperature, the trashing of the house, and the possessed person's great strength. Certainly this film does not portray the Ouija board as a game or toy.

Witchboard is an R-rated horror movie and is available in video, as is its sequel. Advertising for the earlier film reads, "When you open the door to the unknown there's no telling who will drop in . . . or who will drop dead."[46] The device used in the *Witchboard* is a variation of the Ouija board. The video jacket summary states, "College kids playing with a Ouija board make contact [with] an evil spirit named Malfeitor who possesses one of them and drives him to kill." The students are "playing" the board to contact the dead.

Randy Emon called my attention to the third film. "I often wondered why a teen would play with a Ouija board and came to a few conclusions [he mentions peer pressure and curiosity] while others were intrigued with it through the movies such as a recent release called *And You Thought Your Parents Were Weird.*"[47] Emon took his family to see the film without realizing that it featured a variation of the Ouija board called The Oracle. The film appeared in theaters in 1991 and was quickly available for video rental. The video jacket for the film states:

> Get ready for this high-tech comedy adventure where a whiz kid's work is never quite done! Teenagers Josh and Max [actually Max is only ten in the film] Carson spend their free time building a lovable robot named "Newman." Things get a little out of hand when Beth, Josh's beautiful girlfriend, contacts his father's spirit through a Ouija board and ends up landing his ghost in Josh's creation.

The video appears in the family entertainment section of a local Blockbuster Video Store and is also featured on the Disney channel. What message is this "high-tech comedy adventure" communicating? Josh Carson goes to a Halloween party and finds his girlfriend Beth playing the part of a medium on a Ouija board. She tells Josh to try it. When Josh wants to know what it is, a girl bystander tells him it's a telephone to heaven. Beth says, "Come on, put your fingers here and open your mind. Is there anyone you want to contact?" Josh responds, "What? No." Beth then asks twice "Is there anyone who wants to contact Josh Carson?" Suddenly the planchette makes a rapid movement that surprises them. After putting their fingers back on the planchette, it begins to spell out the letters "D-A-D, dad?" Josh mutters, "Very funny"—as he gets up and leaves. Beth says, "Wait Josh, I didn't do anything, I promise." At this point the scene changes to a clear evening sky where a falling star enters the Carson house. This event marks the return of the departed Mr. Carson who takes up residence in a robot.

Mr. Carson reveals himself first to his sons and later to his wife. He credits Beth for his return through her use of the board. When the robot containing Mr. Carson is stolen, the board is used to find out where he is. Albert Einstein is the contact this time. Josh asks, "Dr. Einstein, do you know where my father is?" The disassembled robot is retrieved and reassembled. Mr. Carson tells them, "You have got to let me go back. I belong up there now." With Einstein's help, Mr. Carson returns to heaven.

The film leaves the impression that the board is a benign and successful way to contact dead people who can return to advise and help the living.

Impact on Young Adults. While this section primarily concerns teenagers, there is a legitimate connection between earlier board use and its subsequent impact on young adults— even when that use was not serious or continuous. In my research I discovered an element that recurred again and again—the Ouija often appears to provide correct predictions concerning future events, although it is not infallible. Frequently the board predicts the death of an individual at a particular age or year. While these death dates usually proved to be incorrect, some young people were so disturbed by these prophecies that they became emotionally devastated and some even committed suicide (see chapter 7 for the account of two Swiss girls who committed suicide). In most of these cases, the teenagers continued to be disturbed until the predicted year or age passed. Two examples of this Ouija-originated fear follow.

In a "Dear Abby" letter, a twenty-five-year-old mother of two, writes: "When I was 13, I was fooling around with a Ouija board, when I got a message from my dead grandmother saying she would see me in heaven on my 26th birthday, meaning that I was going to die on that day in an accident." She obviously took the prediction seriously because she told her husband "to marry again soon after" her death so her children would not be "without a mother." She then added, "Abby, for some reason I can't forget it. . . . I only have 11 months to prepare myself if the Ouija board was right. . . . I'm terribly confused and very frightened."[48]

Several years ago a woman wrote to me about her problem.

> In 1963 at a slumber party a bunch of girls (*not* me) asked the question, "Will anyone here die before the year 2000?" The "Board" indicated *I* would in 1997! What really bothers me is that I *haven't* forgotten about the stupid Ouija board, and every so often I think about it! I'm *furious* that I ever give it a thought and that it should bother me at all! Can you help me to NOT worry about it?[49]

This woman is typical of many others who remain psychologically enslaved to a Ouija board prediction—in this case it still bothered her twenty-six years after the event! Of a more serious nature is the spiritual damage that may result from past occult involvement. Neil Anderson writes that his "conferences are full of good Christian people . . . who struggle with victory in their daily lives because they dabbled in the occult during childhood. They have done so innocently out of curiosity or purposely."[50]

*T*his chapter provides numerous examples of the detrimental effects of the Ouija board on children and teenagers. The Ouija board is not just promoted as a game but as a legitimate divination device. Sometimes children or teenagers are encouraged to use the Ouija board to recruit them to other overtly occult practices. In some cases these experiences tremendously affect their lives in later years. This chapter has proved that children and teenagers are especially at risk when they become Ouija users.

Notes _____

1. John Godwin, *Occult America* (Garden City, N.Y.: Doubleday, 1972), 272.
2. Greg Reid, *The Occult Nightmare* (El Paso, Tex.: Youthfire, n.d.), 1.
3. All the information provided in this section comes from *The Missing Princess*, The World of Teddy Ruxpin storybook and cassette (Northridge, Calif.: Alchemy Communications Group, 1985).
4. Patricia Windsor, *How a Weirdo and a Ghost Can Change Your Entire Life* (New York: Delcorte, 1986), copyright page.
5. Ibid., 25–26.
6. Ibid., 53.
7. Ibid., 71.
8. Ibid., 88.
9. Ibid., 122–23.
10. Terry Ann Modica, *The Power of the Occult* (Avon-by-the-Sea, N.J.: Magnificat Press, 1988), 1.
11. Ibid., 1–4.
12. Terry Ann Modica, *The Dark Secret of the Ouija* (Westwood, N.J.: Barbour, 1990).
13. Neil T. Anderson and Steve Russo, *The Seduction of Our Children* (Eugene, Ore.: Harvest House, 1991), 80.
14. "Appendix 1 Summary of Public Hearings: Sessions 1 Through 5," Ontario-Montclair School District, 1987; Committee Report, June 15, 1987.
15. Committee Report, Issue #3.
16. Johanna Michaelsen, *Like Lambs to the Slaughter* (Eugene, Ore.: Harvest House, 1989), 54.
17. Ibid., 61.

18. Berit Kjos, *Your Child and the New Age* (Wheaton, Ill.: Victor, 1990), 27. Douglas Harris of Reachout Trust in Great Britain frequently speaks on the occult in schools. He writes that "there hasn't been a class yet where at least 3 or 4 have not admitted to the fact of playing with Ouija boards and often it is more. There is no question that there is a very overt playing of the Ouija board and an increasing amount of occult activity as well in our schools" (Douglas Harris, letter to the author, Sept. 29, 1992).

   A Sunday school teacher of third and fourth graders in my own church told me she had spent half of a class period with a discussion and questions on the Ouija board. She learned that many students had encountered the board at school or at the homes of friends. In a note she writes, "I was surprised to find that only one of the seven or eight students knew that the Ouija board was at best dangerous and at worst sinful (and this out of a class of regularly churched children). Their curiosity was astonishing." The children asked a number of questions, such as, "Why is it wrong?" "What if I only watch while someone plays with it?" "Why is it dangerous?" The teacher further noted: "I was concerned at how available such things were to children who were unprepared to deal with these dangers. I was concerned by the general tone of their questions, which struck me as, 'How close can I get to the fire without being burned'" (L. G., conversation with author, July 18, 1993 and letter to the author, July 22, 1993).

19. Hans Bender, "Psychosis in the Seance Room," in *The Satan Trap*, ed. Martin Ebon (New York: Doubleday, 1976), 231–38.

20. Stoker Hunt, *Ouija: The Most Dangerous Game* (New York: Barnes and Noble, 1985), 12–13.

21. Ibid., 13.

22. Anderson and Russo, *Seduction*, 34–35.

23. Ibid., 35, 42.

24. State of California's Office of Criminal Justice Planning, Winter 1989–90.

25. Office of Criminal Justice Planning, Research Update (Special Edition), 4, 47.

26. Randy Emon, letter to the author, May 9, 1992.

27. Randy Emon, "Symptoms of Occult Activity Involvement."

28. Randy Emon, letter to the author, Apr. 20, 1992. This letter contained the transcription.

29. Ebon, *The Satan Trap*, ix.

30. Pat Pulling, *The Devil's Web* (Lafayette, La.: Huntington House, 1989), 104.

31. Al Menconi with Dave Hart, *Today's Music: A Window to Your Child's Soul* (Elgin, Ill.: Cook, 1990), 78–79.

32. Chris Willman, "Morrissey Mania at Hollywood Bowl," *Los Angeles Times*, Oct. 12, 1992, p. F-1.

33. "Devil of a Row Over Hit," *The Star* (London), Dec. 7, 1989.
34. Morrissey, "Bona Drag" (New York: Sire Records, 1990). I had no difficultly finding the cassette with "Ouija Board, Ouija Board" at a local music store during the summer of 1993.
35. Greg Reid, *Teen Satanism* (Columbus, Ga.: Quill Publications, 1990), 11–12.
36. Ibid., 13–14.
37. Greg Reid, letter to the author, Sept. 17, 1992.
38. Maureen Davies, *File 18 Newsletter* (October 1989): 1.
39. Sean Sellers, *Web of Darkness* (Tulsa, Okla.: Victory House, 1990), 91. Sellers remains in prison but has now become a Christian.
40. George A. Mather and Larry Nichols, "Doorways to the Demonic," *Lutheran Witness* (October 1987): 5.
41. Michaelsen, *Like Lambs*, 66–67.
42. Anderson and Russo, *Seduction*, 81.
43. John Weldon and Clifford Wilson, *Occult Shock and Psychic Forces* (San Diego, Calif.: Master Books, 1980), ix–x.
44. Larry Jones, letter to the author, Aug. 17, 1992.
45. *Los Angeles Times*, Feb. 21, 1985.
46. *Los Angeles Times* (Calendar), Mar. 8, 1987.
47. Randy Emon, letter to the author, Apr. 20, 1992.
48. *Los Angeles Times*, Feb. 15, 1977.
49. V. S., letter to the author, Apr. 5, 1989.
50. Anderson and Russo, *Seduction*, 32.

7

Court Cases and Newspaper Reports

Both directly and indirectly, the Ouija board has been featured in a number of interesting and sometimes tragic court cases. Many people have had unusual as well as terrifying experiences with the board. Occasionally newspapers report incidents involving the Ouija board and its users, sometimes even warning of its potential dangers.

Court Cases

In chapter 2 we examined the case of *Fuld vs. Fuld* and the Baltimore Talking Board Company's suit against the Internal Revenue Service over the game status of the board. In addition, the board has appeared in a number of other court cases. Several examples are described below.

Twain Copyright Case. On July 28, 1918, the newspaper announced that Harper and Brothers had filed a suit against Mitchell Kennerley, the publisher of *Jap Herron*. Harper and

Brothers, publishers of Samuel Clemens's works and owners of the copyright for the pen name _Mark Twain,_ argued that _Jap Herron_, allegedly dictated by Twain's spirit to Mrs. Hutchings, was clearly inferior to Twain's own books and could hurt his reputation. The novel "according to the introduction, was communicated to Mrs. Emily Grant Hutchings via the Ouija board." Mrs. Hutchings insisted that she and Twain were on a first-name basis.[1]

Secret Burial. An article appeared in February 1921 with the caption "Buried Aged Women Secretly in Garden." The daughter and granddaughter of ninety-one-year-old Nancy Chamberlain disposed of her body in the garden area in back of their house.[2] At the inquest, Mrs. Ruth Townsend, the daughter of the deceased, "declared that 'the first power' had directed her to keep the body of her mother in the house for fifteen days before burying it." And she added, "We enjoyed every minute of it."[3]

When Mrs. Townsend was informed that she was to be committed to "the Psychiatric Hospital until she was rid of religious hallucinations," she broke down, and stated "that the Ouija board was to blame for all of her troubles." She then explained her experiences with the board:

> Marion and I studied with the Ouija board. . . . We started by getting sermons from the beyond. We have hundreds of these sermons that we typewrote and preserved. . . . All of them came from the Ouija board.
>
> Marion did not believe in spirits. I myself was doubtful. But after the Ouija board had been talking to us for days, we just had to believe.[4]

This account illustrates how people can become convinced of the board's power and carefully follow its guidance. Mrs. Townsend was institutionalized in a mental hospital and her daughter went to live with a wealthy family.[5]

117

Cases of Murder or Attempted Murder. On December 27, 1933, the *New York Times* reported the following shocking story:

> SAN DIEGO, Calif., Dec. 26 (AP). Ernest J. Turley, 46 years old, retired naval officer, died in the Naval Hospital here today from gunshot wounds inflicted by his daughter, Mattie, 15. . . .
>
> The daughter testified in an Arizona Juvenile Court that in an Ouija board seance with her mother the board told her to kill her father so her mother . . . "could marry a young cowboy."[6]

The Turleys lived on an Arizona ranch where Mrs. Turley became romantically involved with a cowboy and couldn't decide between him or her husband. She turned to the Ouija board for the answer. Mattie explained what had happened and how she killed her father:

> Mother asked the Ouija board to decide between father and her cowboy friend. As usual, the board moved around at first without meaning but suddenly it spelled out that I was to kill father. It was terrible. I shook all over. Mother asked the Ouija board if the shooting would be successful and it said that it would. . . . We asked what should be used in the shooting and it said a shotgun. . . . We asked about the law, and it said not to fear the law, that everything would turn out all right. We asked how much the insurance would be and it said five thousand dollars. I tried to kill father the next day but I couldn't. I lost my nerve. A few days later, though, I followed him to the corral. I raised the gun and took careful aim between the shoulders but then I lost my nerve again. But I thought of dear mother and what all this would mean to her. I couldn't fail. My hand was trembling awfully but I raised the gun and fired.[7]

Both Mattie and Mrs. Turley were found guilty of murder by an Arizona jury. Mattie drew a six-year sentence at the state school for girls at Randolph. Her mother received a ten- to twenty-five-year prison term, but the higher courts reversed the decision and she was released.[8]

In 1935, Herbert Hurd, a seventy-seven-year-old railroad worker in Kansas City, killed his wife, Nellie. He contended that he was forced to kill her because of the Ouija's influence on her life. Herbert stated "the spirits had told her through her Ouija board that I was too fond of another woman and had given her fifteen thousand dollars of a hidden fortune." Mrs. Hurd had even hired a detective to check on her husband. When his report supported Mr. Hurd's faithfulness, Nellie tried a new tactic—she struck him with a gun, strapped him to a bed, and beat, burned, and tortured him into a false confession. Unable to convince her that the Ouija board had not told the truth and unable to endure her treatment of him, he killed her.[9]

Anderson and Russo relate a more recent case of an unsuccessful murder attempt: "An Arkansas teenager attempted to kill his parents with a club and a butcher knife under the inspiration of a song by the heavy metal band Slayer. The boy said he consulted a Ouija board and heard voices telling him to murder his parents."[10]

Newspaper Reports

Sometimes newspapers report significant incidents of Ouija experimentation,[11] revealing its popularity not only in America but in Europe, especially England.

Student hysteria. Ouija board experimentation also has the potential to affect the behavior of groups of people. The following story appeared in the *New York Times* with the headline "Police Say Hypnosis Test Prompted School Melee."

Students and teachers at a military school here went "berserk" today after a hypnosis demonstration in a science class, the police said.

Harry Cunnill, a police officer said, "Teachers and students were running around tearing up things," after the class. Holes were kicked in walls and doors ripped down at the Miami Aerospace Academy, he said.

None of the 300 students were seriously injured, but one unidentified youth was taken to a hospital after he put his hand through a window, the police said.[12]

How does this case relate to the Ouija board? Just two days later, the real reason for what happened was reported with the headline "Miami School Hysteria Linked to Ouija Board." The article noted that "classes were back to normal at a military school after an outbreak of hysteria attributed at first to hypnosis and later to a Ouija board game." The teacher of the class resigned, "saying that a Ouija board game had got out of control. . . . 'Everybody just got carried away and it was a riot. . . . There were girls screaming that there was a spirit inside' the board."[13]

This type of episode is not unique to America, as the following account illustrates:

> The headmaster of an Essex school was confronted by a dozen terrified 15-year-olds who were seeking help after playing with home-made Ouija boards, a simple device for communicating with outside forces.
>
> Teachers at the school were shocked at the behavior of those involved which included: A 15-year-old boy who stood bolt upright in a geography lesson, shouting at a spirit to get off his shoulder—before he ran out of the classroom and the school.[14]

Bizarre Behavior. In his article on vampires, reporter Daniel St. Albin Greene included the bizarre case of teenager Carl

Johnson who had a compulsion to drink blood. What caused him to have such a revolting urge? "The 'voices' and other eerie stuff began when he and his sister started playing around with a Ouija board a few years ago, he recalls. This led to nightmares, creeping depression, and a suicide attempt." Then Carl began to experience a thirst for blood and even organized a satanic coven. He was so dominated by these compulsions that he feared for his sanity. Attempts to help him were only temporarily successful, and his "voices" and cravings returned. He shared his experience "to warn others that you can be swept away by this kind of thing without realizing it."[15]

Suicides. A London newspaper reported the following tragic account, "Horror of Schoolgirls in a Seance to Suicide." Author John Marshall relates the incident of two girls who lived near Zurich, Switzerland.

> Two schoolgirls who dabbled in the occult killed themselves after a Ouija board said that they would die young.
> The girls, aged 13 and 14, received a message during a seance that they would have tragic lives and die before they reached 18.[16]

The two girls were "holding hands [when they] plunged 200 feet to their deaths." Originally there were three members of the suicide pact, but the third girl decided not to join the others shortly before they jumped.

The girls' school friends stated that the seance participants came to believe in the board's messages because of a realized prediction. "During a seance with the Ouija board the girls believed that one of the [original] quartet would leave the group. . . ." When one girl left because she found a boyfriend, "this made the other three take what they saw in the Ouija board seriously."

Psychic News Warning. The potential dangers of children using the Ouija board are so obvious that even the English *Psy-*

chic News, a noted *spiritualist* newspaper with the world's largest circulation, campaigned against the sale of the board. Roy Stenman's article, "Ouija: the Children's 'Game' that Spells Danger" warned:

> Unless urgent action is taken, thousands of children will find a potentially dangerous psychic "game" in their Christmas stockings this year. Ouija boards, without adequate warning of their dangers, are already in the shops. . . .
>
> The marketing and promotion emphasizes that they are "games." They are on sale alongside snakes and ladders, ludo and other harmless pastimes. In reality they can be mentally hazardous to "play" with. . . .
>
> The mental disturbances that could result from this game have been pointed out to the advertising authorities. A similar approach is now being made to TV companies responsible for carrying the advertisement. . . .
>
> No responsible parent will want to give his child a "toy" that could seriously disturb its mind and possibly plant fears and phobias in the unconscious. A Ouija board is capable of doing this. The manufacturers say that fears about the game are "groundless." They speak with the voice of inexperience. . . .
>
> Simeon Edmunds, an SPR [Society for Psychical Research] member, expressing a personal opinion, told me [the reporter] last week: "Any responsible person, whatever his views on the origin of Ouija board messages, would be in agreement that this is not a game for children."
>
> Edmunds added that he knew of "a number of cases where very real harm had been done" by playing with Ouija boards.[17]

The article included the story of a fourteen-year-old school girl who believed that she had contacted a spirit claiming to have been killed during the reign of Charles I. She was instructed to go with a friend to a nearby town where they were to dig up the spirit's guns and money. The girl then pleaded, "I must go because if I don't something awful will happen to me. PLEASE help me. I am a bit upset at this idea. My friend is to come with me. And we are both to take spades (on a train!)."[18]

The article concludes:

> We appeal to Waddingtons [the manufacturers] to think again, and withdraw this "toy" from the market. We appeal also to the Minister of Health to inquire into the harmful mental effects of the "game," before any damage results.
>
> In the interests of children and teenagers everywhere, this must be done now.[19]

Cat Sacrifice. A short article in a London paper reported the sacrificial burning of a cat. Detectives questioned teenagers about the "charred remains of the cat found on a beach in Clevedon, Bristol. The animal may have been staked out over an open fire." The headmaster of Clevedon comprehensive school said that he believed some of the students "'have been involved in the fringes of a group of both youngsters and adults who take part in satanic activities.' Police said that several pupils became involved with Ouija boards and then took it a step further."[20]

A "Haunting" Case. The *L.A. Times* reported the experiences of Jackie Hernandez and her two-year-old son.[21] Jackie separated from her husband in the winter of 1988–89. The haunting experiences began after she moved into a San Pedro bungalow. The most unusual feature of this case is that the haunting continued wherever she went, even after she moved to Kern County. "The ordeal, Hernandez says, was a Grade A waking nightmare replete with strange lights, colored mists, apparitions, and stinking blood-like liquid oozing from the walls." The phenomena "began slowly. . . . The cat chased eerie shadows around the house; voices muttered in the attic . . . she saw pencils fly out of a pencil holder. She thought she was hallucinating, perhaps because of her pregnancy." But after her daughter's birth, she saw an apparition of a "gnarled old man" and had a nightmare in which she experienced the death struggle of a murder victim.

Parapsychologist Barry Taff has investigated some three thousand cases of the supernatural, many of which turned out to be fraudulent. Hernandez invited him to visit the San Pedro residence and the Kern County trailer with his investigative crew. Taff concluded that something out of the ordinary was taking place.

The article mentions Ouija board use twice. "Hernandez and friends say that they established, via an Ouija board, a possible link with a 60-year-old suspicious death, perhaps the killing Jackie dreamed about." In the fall of 1989 Jackie Hernandez returned to her husband and moved to Kern County. The reconciliation attempt failed after a few months, her husband left, and the phenomena began again. Taff and his assistants again visited the trailer, which led to the second Ouija board use. When they arrived, they

> entered what Hernandez describes as a maelstrom. For starters, the researchers could not get their video cameras to work—something kept switching off the equipment.
>
> Partly in desperation, she suggested that the investigators try the Ouija board. As they began, she recalls, their table began to shake. And the session ended when photographer Wheatcraft was thrown against the trailer wall by an invisible force.

Hernandez believes that the Ouija's message about the suspicious death was the reason for the supernatural phenomena. In the summer of 1990 Hernandez moved back to Los Angeles to live in a friend's house and the manifestations have tapered off. "In the last year or so, Hernandez claims to have experienced only infrequent visitations." The article does not indicate the frequency of Hernandez's Ouija use or if she used it before the manifestations in the San Pedro bungalow began.

Six AWOL Intelligence Specialists. This case is sometimes known as the case of "The Gulf Stream Six." Reports of this incident are often sensationalized and inaccurate. The area of Gulf Breeze, Florida, has been described "as a hotbed of flying saucer sightings."[22] The editor and publisher of the *Gulf Breeze Sentinel* estimated "that in the past 2 1/2 years, he's heard of UFO sightings from at least 200 people, including his parents." We will focus on the arrest of "six young soldiers, AWOL from their top secret Army posts in Augsburg, West Germany. According to friends, the soldiers had come here to witness the end of the world."[23]

Jacques Vallee discusses this case in his book *Revelations*. "It is on July 9, 1990, three weeks before the invasion of Kuwait by Saddam Hussein, that six U.S. Army Intelligence specialists deserted their posts in Augsburg, Germany."[24] On the night of July 13, one of the six soldiers was stopped by a Gulf Breeze police officer because of a broken taillight. A computer check revealed that the man was wanted by the Army. Shortly afterwards, the remaining five soldiers were located—four at the home of Anna Foster, a friend of one of the soldiers. She was a psychic who worked at a New Age bookstore.[25]

Vallee explains what happened after their arrest:

> The six soldiers were quickly moved back behind the fence at Fort Benning, Georgia, where they were interrogated [for three days] by Army Intelligence, CIA, and NSA. . . .
>
> From Fort Benning the six deserters were quickly transferred to Fort Knox, and a remarkable series of events was set into motion. The army sim-

ply cleared them in a routine espionage investigation, issued them general discharges, and turned them loose![26]

Vallee questions whether "psychic messages received by Vance A. Davis," one of the soldiers, was the real reason that the men went AWOL. He asks, "Is it plausible that six smart soldiers—they may have been deluded, but they certainly demonstrated that they were not stupid—would have taken such a radical step as desertion purely on the basis of telepathic impressions?"[27] Vance Davis claims that "Vallee did not contact us to check out our story."[28]

What is the Ouija board's role in this series of events? The answer appeared in the Associated Press release some two years after their discharge. The headline in the Eureka *Times Standard* reads, "Six went AWOL at Ouija's Orders." Vance Davis was the source for the A.P. story. He claims that the newspaper articles claiming the soldiers went to Gulf Breeze to await the "Second Coming of Christ in a UFO," were untrue. Actually the soldiers went to Gulf Breeze to visit a friend and were unaware of its UFO notoriety.[29]

Davis states "the reason they left their Army intelligence posts was quite simple: Ouija board spirits told them they were needed to help lead the world through an impending cataclysm." The group was also informed that others would aid them in their task. After remaining silent for two years, "Davis now says he wants to tell his story to set the record straight and because, according to the Ouija board, race riots in Los Angeles were to be a signal the group should go public."[30]

Davis explains that their Ouija board experimentation began "innocently in November 1989" after other psychic approaches had failed. "Davis says the members of the group 'hit brick walls' until finally they tried a Ouija board. 'Someone showed up,' he says, 'I'm talking spiritually.'"[31]

According to Davis, the board predicted the beginning of the Gulf War and the "1990 Iran earthquake." It even predicted that Saddam Hussein would be a "thorn in the side" of the United States two years after the war was over and gave a number of other details.[32]

Davis further noted,

> At the end of May we were told we might think about trying to get out of the service because there's going to be some serious things occurring in the next five years, and being in the service would not help us grow and become what we were supposed to become.[33]

So all six soldiers made the decision to return to the United States. Davis emphasizes that this was *their* decision, not the Ouija board's.

In my interviews with Davis I learned that the spirits told him that the Ouija board communication was necessary because the participants would not listen in any other way. The soldiers used the commercial Parker Brothers board. Two of them regularly worked the board and two recorded the message in written form and on a tape recorder. At first the planchette moved slowly, but then it became normal for it to move so quickly ("lightning speed") that they could barely keep up with it, and sometimes they could not. There were a total of nine to ten sessions over an eight-month period, lasting as long as thirteen hours, or as few as seven. Davis was interested in the paranormal before they began experimenting, and it was at his instigation that they tried the Ouija board. Davis had never used a board before and wanted to prove or disprove that it worked.

Davis claims that they experienced the difference between "good" and "evil" spirits. There was a definite "energy" change when a presence entered the room. The spirits communicated their messages with perfect spelling and in context; often the messages were quite complex. The spirits identified themselves as an old lady from Selma, Alabama, and as the apostles John and Timothy. The apostles frequently quoted from the New Testament; the soldiers checked the quotations against the Bible for accuracy.

By the time the soldiers left their post at Augsburg, they had collected about two hundred pages of Ouija notes. When they were arrested, the army seized these notes and never returned them. The six soldiers remain good friends today. They came from different religious backgrounds—one even began as an atheist, but his Ouija experience changed his mind.

What role has the Ouija board played in Davis's life since that time? Davis replied, "I don't want to touch the board again. I don't need it. I haven't worked the Ouija board since the experience." Would he recommend the Ouija board to others? He emphatically answered, "No, especially not for children or young people."[34] This case demonstrates yet another instance where Ouija communications were taken so seriously that they irrevocably changed the lives of the participants.

The court cases and newspaper articles in this chapter illustrate the startling impact the Ouija board can have on the users' lives. These experiences also serve as a warning of the consequences of Ouija experimentation.

Notes

1. *New York Times*, July 28, 1918, III, p. 3.
2. *New York Times*, Feb. 17, 1921, p. 32.
3. *New York Times*, Feb. 18, 1921, p. 2.
4. *New York Times*, Feb. 20, 1921, p. 16.
5. Ibid.
6. *New York Times*, Dec. 27, 1933, p. 40.
7. Paul Sann, *Fads, Follies, and Delusions of the American People* (New York: Crown, 1967), 143.
8. *New York Times*, Dec. 27, 1933, p. 40; Jan. 17, 1934, p. 6; Sann, *Fads*, 143.
9. Sann, *Fads*, 143.
10. Neil Anderson and Steve Russo, *The Seduction of Our Children* (Eugene, Ore.: Harvest House, 1991), 91–92.
11. Newspaper articles about Ouija cases are sometimes cited in other materials, but I have only included cases in this section that I have copies of or have examined.
12. *New York Times*, Oct. 26, 1979, p. A-16.

13. *New York Times,* Oct. 28, 1979, p. 26.

14. *Doorways to Danger* (London: Evangelical Alliance, 1987), 6.

15. "It's Only Superstition, Right? Real Vampires," *National Observer,* June 1, 1974, pp. 1, 16.

16. *Daily Express,* Oct. 26, 1990. The quotation and the following account all appear in this article.

17. Roy Stemman, "Ouija: the Children's Game That Spells Dangers," *Psychic News,* Sept. 21, 1968, p. 1.

18. Ibid., 1, 8. Rev. Russell Parker, field officer of The Acorn Christian Healing Trust in Great Britain, observes: "Spiritists do not actually give a proper reason why the spirits of the Ouija board are wrong and the spirits of their own practice are acceptable. It is based purely on the awareness of the bad effects of the Ouija board. There is no theological reasoning given" (Russell Parker, letter to the author, Nov. 8, 1992).

19. Ibid., 8.

20. *Daily Mail,* Feb. 6, 1990, p. 2.

21. The quotes and summary in the following account come from an article by Garry Abrams, "Tangled Tales from the Crypt?" *Los Angeles Times* Mar. 23, 1993, pp. E-1, 2.

22. *Los Angeles Times,* Aug. 6, 1990, pp. E-1, 4.

23. Ibid., 1.

24. Jacques Vallee, *Revelations* (New York: Ballentine, 1991), 188.

25. Ibid.; Vance Davis, telephone interviews with the author, Sept. 10, 1992; Sept. 21, 1992; Jan. 20, 1993.

26. Vallee, *Revelations,* 189–90.

27. Ibid., 191. Davis claims that the following statement from Vallee is untrue and it is based on newspaper reports that were in error. "They had left their posts, it now appeared, in the burning belief that Armageddon was imminent . . . that they had been designated to greet alien spaceships marking the return of Jesus Christ. . . . One of the objectives of their trip to Gulf Breeze was to find the Antichrist and kill him" (*Revelations,* 189).

28. Davis interviews.

29. Associated Press release, July 19, 1992 in the Eureka *Times Standard* (undated); Davis interviews.

30. Eureka *Times Standard.*

31. Ibid.

32. Ibid.; Davis interviews.

33. Ibid.

34. Davis interviews. This case was featured on TV's "Inside Edition" on Sept. 7, 1992. In some areas it aired the next day. Another treatment appeared on "Sightings" (Fox TV) on Feb. 12, 1993.

8

The Exorcist
and Other Cases

Although William Peter Blatty's novel *The Exorcist* (1971) and
film (1973) are over two decades old, they still fascinate the
general public. As recently as the summer of 1993, the book
Possessed: The True Story of an Exorcism, by Thomas B. Allen
appeared. Following the publication of *The Exorcist,* Blatty revealed that his book was based on a true story that occurred
near Georgetown University in 1949. In my correspondence
with Blatty, he confirmed that "the book is based on a true
story, and the involvement with demon possession was
through the Ouija board."[1] The Ouija board? Ed Warren, a
noted authority on possession, stresses:

> The Ouija board has proven to be a notorious passkey
> to terror, even when the intent of communication is
> decidedly positive in nature. . . . Of the cases we re-
> spond to, four in ten concern individuals who have
> raised inhuman spirits using a Ouija board. I was one
> of the few people who examined the official records

of *The Exorcist* case. . . . And do you know how it originally got started? By using a Ouija board![2]

This chapter will examine the true story behind *The Exorcist*, Blatty's treatment of the Ouija board and demon possession, and three other true accounts of Ouija board use.

The Story Behind The Exorcist

In August 1949 a news item in the *Catholic Review* of Washington, D.C., reported the successful exorcism of a fourteen-year-old boy. No other information was provided. Washington *Evening Star* reporter Jeremiah O'Leary noticed the item and attempted to interest two of his editors in the story, but to no avail. One editor commented: "Junior, there are some things it's better to stay away from. I wouldn't touch it with a ten-foot pole. But if you want it done, do it yourself."[3] In three days O'Leary uncovered the story's details and submitted his article, but the editors rejected it. Finally, he approached the managing editor of the newspaper who published the article on August 19, but placed it on page B-3—"a good place to hide a controversial story in those days," said O'Leary.[4]

The day after O'Leary's article appeared, the story hit the front page of the *Washington Post* and was picked up by other wire services, when it became front-page news across the country.[5] Bill Brinkley's *Washington Post* article stated that the case was "perhaps one of the most remarkable experiences of its kind in recent religious history." As a junior at Georgetown University, William Blatty read this article and became fascinated by the topic. While writing a research paper on demon possession during his senior year, Blatty obtained a copy of the priest's journal with the account of the exorcism. This later became the outline for Regan's actions in *The Exorcist*. Blatty kept a copy of the Jesuit's journal but promised not to release it.[6]

The actual boy in this case was identified by one source

as Douglass Deen,[7] the fourteen-year-old son of a Lutheran mechanic who lived in Mount Rainier, Maryland, on the outskirts of Washington, D.C. The phenomena began with strange sounds like dripping water and scratching from the walls and attic of the Deen house on the night of January 15, 1949.[8] As in *The Exorcist*, the family suspected that rodents caused the noises and employed an exterminator, "but no trace of rats or other rodents was found."[9] The manifestations quickly grew worse.[10] Occasionally the family saw dishes and other objects fly through the air and furniture move across the room or heard the sound of footsteps.[11] Finally the terrified family visited their minister, "Rev. Winston," to report the strange phenomena in their home and to enlist his aid.[12] Although Winston witnessed these impressive manifestations, he remained skeptical because he believed the boy was somehow the cause.[13]

On February 17, Winston invited the boy to spend the night in his home and he and the boy retired to a bedroom with twin beds. The room was quiet for about ten minutes, but then the boy's bed began to vibrate and they heard scraping and scratching noises from the wall. The minister turned on the light to see what was happening. There was no possible natural explanation for what he observed. He had seen the same manifestations in the boy's home.[14]

The minister then placed the boy in a heavy armchair. The boy drew his knees up under his chin with his body wrapped up in a blanket. As the minister watched, the chair moved several inches until it reached the wall and could go no further—then it began to tip in the opposite direction. The boy cried out, "It's going over with me, Pastor." He was thrown to the floor.[15] Since it was obvious that neither of them could get any sleep with the bed's violent vibrations, Winston improvised a bed on the floor using a pillow and two blankets. The boy soon dropped off to sleep.

With the lights still on, Rev. Winston lay upon his own bed, continuing to watch the boy. Now the bedding, and the boy, began to slide slowly across the room. The pallet moved under the beds. The lad was awakened when his head bumped against a far bedpost.

The minister remade the pallet immediately but to no purpose. This time, the pallet, boy and all, whipped around in a half circle on the floor. Then it slid under the bed again.

In both instances the boy's hands were outside the bedding, his body was rigid, and there was no wrinkling of the blankets.[16]

On different occasions, skeptical neighbors "invited the boy and his mother to spend a night in their 'unhaunted' homes, only to have some of the manifestations—such as the violent, apparently involuntary shakings of the boy's bed—happen before their eyes."[17] The boy's aunt later recounted what happened at her home when the boy lay down on a bed:

All of a sudden the mattress starts going, just raised up in the air, up and down, up and down, and my sister hollered for me, so I ran in and tried to help and said there was nothing in that room that could harm us, and said to my nephew, I'm gonna lay down with you and there isn't anybody gonna bother us, and oh, I'll tell you that mattress just raised *both* of us right up in the air. We both flew off and my nephew started out of the bedroom. I happened to have a table up against the wall with a vase of flowers on it and I got out but as my nephew tried to leave, that table actually flew in front of the door and would not let him out.[18]

In Blatty's book, *I'll Tell Them I Remember You,* he recalls that

at the outset of the boy's possession syndrome, it was stated by Jesuits on the campus, the boy, according to his mother, was leaning over in the bathroom, washing his face above the sink, when the mother saw a word rise up in flesh upon his back. The poltergeist activity was then in full swing. The mother shrieked in hysteria, "Who is it? Stop it! Who's doing these things?" The word, an obscenity, gave way to TILLY. Tilly was an aunt of the boy, now deceased. She had allegedly "communicated" with the family through the use of a Ouija board some time before. Now the mother shouted, "What do you want?" went the story. The answer was GO. "Go where?" And here the word LOUIS appeared. No more answers appeared after that.[19]

Blatty also notes the strange experience of the Lutheran minister and a priest who were assigned to investigate the case. When they visited the boy's house, "both men, as they entered, were knocked flat to the ground by what they later described as an 'invisible force.'"[20] Eventually, the boy's affliction was studied exhaustively at two Jesuit hospitals—one at Georgetown University and the other at St. Louis University. Later that year *Post* reporter Bill Brinkley interviewed a priest involved in the case who stated that before the exorcism was undertaken, "all medical and psychiatric means of curing the boy . . . were exhausted."[21]

Blatty enumerated the various manifestations that occurred during the course of the exorcism:

Among the bizarre phenomena . . . were "brandings"—lines and markings, some single, some double and even triple, that resembled clawmarks and appeared spontaneously on the flesh of the boy each day and as many as thirty times in the day. Their appearance was accompanied in every instance by screams of anguish and pain from the boy.

Once, when the exorcist was sitting on the bed no more than two feet from the boy, a branding appeared even as he watched. It extended from the boy's inner thigh to his ankle. Near the ankle the skin was broken and droplets of blood appeared. Sometimes the brandings were images and words. Some of the words that appeared were SPITE, HELL and EXIT.[22]

For a period of two months, Rev. William Bowdern, the priest in charge of the boy's case, remained with the boy wherever he went, and even slept in the same house, sometimes in the same room.[23] During this time the priest also

witnessed many of the same manifestations reported by the Protestant minister this month [Aug. 1949] to a closed meeting of the Society of Parapsychology. It was at this session that Dr. J. B. Rhine, director of the famed parapsychology laboratory at Duke University, who came here to study the case, was quoted as saying it was "the most impressive" poltergeist (noisy ghost) phenomenon that had come to his attention in his years of celebrated investigation in the field.[24]

Other manifestations of possession in this case include: raucous blasphemies, obscene behavior, vomiting and urinating, near super-human strength, and clairvoyance concerning the personal affairs of those around him.[25] In addition, "The boy broke into a violent tantrum of screaming, cursing and voicing of Latin phrases—a language he had never studied" when the climax to the ritual of exorcism was reached and the demon was commanded to depart.[26]

The process of deliverance was lengthy and difficult. During the ordeal, the exorcist Bowdern underwent a "black fast" of bread and water and lost more than forty pounds.[27] The process of exorcism took approximately two months and twenty to thirty performances of the rite (each about forty-five minutes in length).[28] The final exorcism was performed in May, when the "possessing spirit identified himself as one of the fallen angels mentioned in the Bible and then departed." The manifestations ceased.[29] The boy attended a Catholic high school and Georgetown University. Apparently he had no recollection of what happened to him. He later married and became the father of three children.[30]

Was the boy really demon possessed? The doctors at the two Catholic hospitals, various Catholic authorities, and other specialists were unable to help the boy through medical or psychiatric means. The parents exhausted every possible medical or psychiatric avenue before they turned to the ritual of exorcism. This seemed the only avenue open to them. Permission to use the ritual is granted only when there is strong physical, emotional, and spiritual evidence of demon possession.

> Use of the ritual is rare in the western Christian world, as are reported cases of diabolical possession. Never is permission to employ the ritual granted except where an afflicted person's case has been fully documented as being a bona fide one.[31]

William Friedkin, director of *The Exorcist*, spent almost a year researching for the film before shooting began. His information and reaction on the case are interesting.

> This particular boy in the 1949 case on which the film was based met all the requirements for exorcism as set forth by the church. He was speaking in a voice not his own, a language not his own. He was possessed of superhuman powers. He broke the arm of the priest performing the exorcism [and another priest's nose]. His bed shook up and down. . . .
>
> The priest spent the night in the room on a mat that slid all over the floor. The furniture tried to attack him. A bottle jumped off the wall and broke the tiles on the floor at his feet and yet the bottle didn't break. The boy would vomit strange-smelling fluids. Doctors, psychiatrists, everyone they could get, ex-

amined him and nobody could figure out what was wrong. So what I believe is that this boy was suffering from a disease for which there was and is no name. It was demonic possession. . . .

The original exorcism was performed at a hospital in St. Louis. It didn't happen in someone's house or in a church or some place private where someone might've been carried away. Doctors and nurses were in attendance and I have a day-to-day account of what happened. It's the most incredible thing I have ever known.[32]

An editorial in the Jesuit publication *America* shortly after the case noted that "it seems certain that the boy manifested all the classical signs of real diabolical possession."[33] Occasionally people try to explain this case as one of paranoid schizophrenia. Blatty counters with the following experience: "The fact is I do not know of any mental disorder that can make a bedside table levitate up to the ceiling as happened with this boy."[34] In Blatty's book, *I'll Tell Them I Remember You,* he notes: "A professor of physics from the University of Washington reportedly had seen the boy's bedside table in the hospital 'float up to the ceiling, hover, then come down.'"[35] If this really happened, and it does not seem strange in the light of the other unusual occurrences in the case, certainly any purely naturalistic explanation of the case is inadequate.

Years later Bowdern wrote Blatty about the case. Bowdern remained convinced that this incident was an actual case of possession. Blatty concurred with this conclusion and told interviewer Charles Champlin, "If I didn't believe in possession, I wouldn't have written the book."[36]

The Role of the Ouija Board in The Exorcist

People who read *The Exorcist* and the writers who review it often miss the role the Ouija board played in Regan's possession. The film's portrayal of the Ouija board and the surprising physical manifestations and possession that resulted from its use accurately reflect actual cases of Ouija use that have been verified by researchers and experts in the field of occult investigation.

In the novel Chris MacNeil, the mother of Regan, acquires the Ouija board as a "possible means of exposing clues to her subconscious." She uses the board on several occasions with different friends, but without much success. Once, when she uses the board with film director Burke Dennings, he consciously manipulates the planchette. Chris loses interest in the board and even forgets that she has one. Chris's daughter Regan begins "playing" with the board by herself. She contacts a spirit who calls himself "Captain Howdy"—an apparently friendly spirit. Ouija communications frequently begin with messages from good or friendly spirits, but later these spirits become anything but nice.[37] Early in the novel Regan spends considerable time alone with the Ouija board and grows increasingly involved with it. One night when Chris gives a dinner party, she goes down to the playroom to put Regan to bed and finds the child playing with the Ouija board. "She seemed sullen; abstracted; remote."[38] Regan's progressive withdrawal is symptomatic of deepening Ouija involvement.

After the party Chris asks the psychic Mrs. Perrin about Regan's use of the board. She replies: "I would take it away from her."[39] She then warns that dabbling with the occult "can be dangerous. And that includes fooling around with a Ouija board."[40] Chris responds that the Ouija board just reflects a person's subconscious—a common attitude toward the board.[41] Mrs. Perrin's admits that it "could be suggestion,"

> but in story after story that I've heard about seances, Ouija boards, *all* of that, they always seem to point to the opening of a door of some sort. . . . All I know is that things seem to happen. And, my dear, there are lunatic asylums all over the world filled with people who dabbled in the occult.[42]

Regan's progressive control by "Captain Howdy" displays the hallmarks of possession—a complete inability to resist the demon's domination. Chris explains Regan's deteriorating condition to Dr. Klein and tells him that Regan can now communicate directly with "Captain Howdy" *without* the board—"now she could hear him."[43] This ability to communicate directly with the spirit after a period of Ouija board use is fairly symptomatic of real Ouija use.

The information about the Ouija board contained in *The Exorcist* is accurate and can be verified both by the cases in the present volume and by many others. From the Christian perspective, the use of the Ouija board must be *totally avoided*—it offers the demonic an opportunity to control its users.

Demon Possession

Is *The Exorcist's* nightmarish account of the symptoms of demon possession believable? Some symptoms of possession have been accurately recorded and observed for centuries all over the world. Many of Regan's symptoms were specifically patterned after the actual case of the Mount Rainier boy's experience. Blatty also relied heavily on T. K. Oesterreich's classic study, *Possession*, which was first published in 1921.[44]

In *Casting Out the Devils*, Francoise Strachan summarizes the symptoms of possession as recorded in material obtained from practicing exorcists and other informed sources. For one who has read *The Exorcist*, Strachan's summary reads like a review of many of Regan's symptoms and experiences.

> There are many and varying degrees of possession. . . . Yet long established cases show many and varied symptoms: a wasting of the frame, a distention of the stomach. The features usually express hatred, anger, insult, mockery, and at the same time the organic functions are affected by contractions and spasms of the entrails. Sometimes the complexion alters, there

can be distressing symptoms of nausea, vomiting, furred tongue and foul breath. The action of the entrails causes sensations of great pain and anguish, often aggravated by irritations of the skin and mucous membrane. The victim explains his anguish by the presence of an animal or a devil which is constantly moving inside his stomach, biting, pinching, burning, and torturing him in every possible way. He can also be subject to dizziness, headaches and various sensations which seem to have some exterior cause, such as violent pains in the nape of the neck, which the victim imagines to have been occasioned by a blow, and pains in the spine which he attributes to the same cause. Also twitchings, cramps, impressions of swelling, and varying states of tension which the victim interprets as marking the entrance of the devil into his body or the moment of his leaving it.

Sometimes there are accompanying smells such as dead flowers, or excess perspiration, and in very severe cases there is an unpleasant smell of sickness or diarrhea. There can be changes also in the voice. It can become deep, menacing, or sardonic, mocking the most innocent bystander, and using filthy words quite against the victim's usual practice. Sometimes automatic writing will appear suddenly in a page of ordinary writing, and the pen snatched and flung into the middle of the room. In very advanced cases of possession the demon literally dominates the body, seizes on the organs and uses them as if they were his own. It can actuate the nervous system and produce movements in the limbs, speaking perhaps, through the patient's mouth. This is not the same as mediumship, the difference being that the possessed person has a violent character with an accompanying repugnant nature. Also possession is compulsive; whereas with mediumship, free will is involved.[45]

Ed and Lorraine Warren, recognized as "the nation's foremost demonologists" with forty-three years of on-site experience in North America, Europe, and Australia, have investigated over three thousand cases of demon possession.[46] The following accounts from the Warrens correlate Ouija board use to dramatic manifestations of demonic activity. Each case has been observed by a number of witnesses. The Enfield and Donovan cases in *The Demonologist* are attested by author Gerald Brittle: "Great care has been taken . . . to include only those cases in the Warrens' files that were witnessed by ordained clergymen and exorcists, or in lesser circumstances, where the principles were credible and reliable and their comments are plainly recorded on tape. It also should be stressed that there is no exaggeration or hyperbole in the presentation of the phenomena." The Warrens' "experiences have been proven and documented by priests, rabbis, doctors, mediums, police, and recognized experts in psychic research."[47] Ed Warren explains how the board functions as a dangerous open door.

> The Ouija is nothing by itself. . . . It's just a pressed piece of board with the alphabet on it. The same effect can be had with an upside-down wine glass on a waxed table. . . . But in either case, it is a medium for communication. In other words, it's what you use the object *for*. When you use the Ouija board, you give permission for an unknown spirit to communicate with you. Would you open the front door to your house and let in anyone who felt like it? Of course not. Yet that's exactly what you're doing on a supernatural level. . . . As we've said many times, doors have got to be opened before most of this activity can occur. The Ouija board is one way to do it.[48]

The case of demonic manifestation in Enfield, England,[49] occurred over a three-year period. The occult phenomena started in August 1977, but the case actually "began in 1976, when two girls drew inhuman entities into the house after playing with . . . a Ouija board. The girls had no sinister purposes in using it: they simply had nothing else to do, and were playing with the board as a game." Ed explains that the original spirit brought in others.

> When the spirits were first drawn in, the usual run of infestation phenomena erupted: knockings, rappings, scratchings, poundings and so forth. As time went on, the phenomena upgraded. Objects materialized, people levitated—especially the girls—and a number of black forms manifested and floated around the house at night.[50]

Ed visited the Enfield house on a number of occasions. During his first visit, he interviewed the family members individually and as a group—the divorced mother, the two girls, and a younger brother. He concluded from his observations there was a supernatural character to the incidents. "For example, the girls would levitate off the floor, *crisscross* in the air, and then be set back down again in a display of inhuman power." Levitation occurred a number of times. "Even as [Ed] talked with the family, things would rise up in the air and float around the room. One evening a wooden chair lifted up in the air, stayed still for a moment, then exploded." At another time a softball-sized rock materialized and crashed to the floor. Even more serious phenomena occurred when the girls came "under episodes of possession"— their facial features changed and they exhibited great strength. One of the girls tried to kill the mother a number of times. But as Ed explains:

> By far, though, the most compelling aspect to this case is the physicalized voice manifestations that occur in the house. The voices of six different spirits talk out loud *in the room*. It's as though there were six invisible people present. It's incredible: you can't believe it even when you're there![51]

Ed taped over three hours of the voices and played them for author Gerald Brittle, who describes them as "something truly incredible." Along with the voices, "fully ten percent of the recording is taken up with grunts, moans, 'yeccchs,' and the imitation of animal sounds, of which the most often repeated is that of a barking dog." The British Society for Psychical Research made a thorough investigation of the case and determined that the voices and sounds could not be "projected by loudspeakers or by any other electronic means." A two-way conversation was established between the spirits and the people in the house. Brittle provides several pages of Warren's recorded interrogation, primarily with the spirit "Fred."

> All the while I was talking to these spirits . . . things were flying around the room. That's what those crashing and bumping sounds are in the background. Chairs and tables were lifting and dropping. Small, little objects would whiz across the room and bounce off the wall. In the dining room, the wallpaper was peeling away from the walls as we watched. A butcher knife materialized in the lap of my assistant, Paul. A nail was produced out of thin air. And, as has come to be expected in the house, the spirits left a pile of excrement on the mother's bedroom carpet upstairs at three in the afternoon.
>
> When the spirits on the recording weren't going through a fit of random insanity, they seemed to amuse themselves by filling the room with grunts, quacks, barks, shrieks, and a variety of other animal sounds—the most annoying being that of a shrill, screeching cat.[52]

The Enfield spirit manifestations were still present at the time Warren was interviewed by Brittle.

Another case investigated by the Warrens concerned a fifteen-year-old girl (they call her Cindy McBain).[53] For amusement, Cindy regularly frequented a shopping mall with her friends because she did not date. One Saturday as she was browsing through an antique store, she spotted an old Ouija board. It piqued her curiosity so she bought it and took it home. She spent several months experimenting with the board with no result, but one day as she was working it with her girlfriend, they both became aware of a presence. "Cindy did in fact hear a vague rasping noise . . . from *inside* the wall." The noise continued and sounded like "something scratching to get out" and became "more and more like a clawing." Cindy's friend became frightened and decided to leave, but first she warned Cindy to "get rid of that board."

Cindy failed to heed this warning and became even more involved with the board. Her friends were concerned by her withdrawal and loss of appetite. After four months of Ouija use, her mother began to hear noises from Cindy's bedroom. What she "seemed to be hearing were the sounds of people making love." Because she did not want to believe this was actually happening, she accepted her husband's explanation that Cindy was singing aloud with her music tapes. Finally the mother entered the room and found "Cindy on her bed with the headphones on, listening to music." There was no one else there. And then she "saw how much weight she'd lost, how dark the circles were under her eyes, how she'd taken to biting her nails until they were bloody." Then the mother spotted the Ouija board for the first time, but when she asked the daughter about it, she was rebuffed. She reached for the board, but Cindy slapped her hand away. Her second attempt to take the board also failed. "For the first time in my life, I was afraid of my daughter." Later Cindy's father experienced the same response.

The following three weeks were like a horrible nightmare. "The clawing in the walls became so pronounced that it could be heard throughout the house" and "the sound of sexual ecstasy emanating from Cindy's room could now be heard as far away as the formal dining room." The daughter became a "virtual stranger" to her parents with swinging moods of rage and sobbing. As Cindy became more with-drawn, her parents consulted a minister, a priest, and a psy-chiatrist, but none of them were able to help her. The father attempted to seize the board to destroy it, but Cindy attacked him "slapping him viciously, slamming his head into the wall again and again." Later the board was nowhere to be found—she had hidden it.

"In two more weeks, after three sessions with a psychi-atrist, Cindy McBain was taken to a psychiatric hospital" and this is where Ed and Lorraine Warren met her. They observed that even after being given tranquilizers "she still flew into rages." Somehow she sneaked the Ouija board into her hos-pital room and continued to work it. The Warrens discovered that Cindy and some of her friends had purchased occult books and were experimenting with "oaths and rituals they'd found in the books."

Mrs. McBain told the Warrens and Father Elemi, who now accompanied them, "that she herself had seen a black shape moving down the upstairs hallway one day. The shape seemed to be composed of black fog. It had gone into Cindy's room." After hearing this information, Ed said "any doubts we'd had about demonic infestation and possession were gone now."

After a brief visit with the girl resulted in a demonic re-sponse, the Warrens prepared for an exorcism. When the ex-orcism began, further demonic manifestations appeared in the girl and in the room. The girl "writhed on the bed" and screamed. When the priest addressed the demon, "the demon responded in an angry voice. . . . Loud thumping sounds came from inside the wall. A fetid odor filled the room. You had to cover your mouth and nose." Cindy screamed ob-scenities, threw things at the wall, and "moved around on the bed as if taking some kind of sexual pleasure, and fi-nally," she "lay still on the bed." The exorcism was complete in about one hour.

Cindy spent another four days in the hospital before she went home, but she required rehospitalization three weeks later when the demon reappeared (or, "had it just been lay-ing dormant"?). Ed concludes, "Cindy, now a young woman, leads a somewhat normal life—but she is always subject to what her doctor calls 'attacks.' He calls it mental illness. But we know better."

*P*atty Donovan[54] was a teenager who was raised in a strict and religious family. But early in 1974, she became lonely and bored, so she "decided to try to find a friend on the Ouija board." She gave her name and asked if a spirit was pres-ent—"suddenly the planchette whizzed up to YES." What be-gan innocently enough become an addiction as Patty con-tacted the same presence each night. The spirit complimented her and played on feelings of loneliness. Patty rehearsed the events of her day to the spirit and "the spirit responded with stories about its death, and how lonely it had been before 'meeting' her." Over a period of several months, Patty began to believe that her contact was the spirit of a teenage boy. The spirit refused to reveal its name, claiming that it was not al-lowed to do so. Patty "became infatuated with the spirit on the Ouija board, which she came to view as a boyfriend." The spirit gave her information about trivial events in the future that later came true. "After a year of trading intimacies on the board, Patty became emotionally dependent on the spirit."

About a year after the first contact, in late February Patty asked if the spirit could tell her about her future. (What the spirit predicted for the next six years did happen.) Next, "she craved to *see* her invisible boyfriend. Late Saturday night, March 2, she pleaded for him to manifest. Just once, she told the spirit, she wanted to see what he looked like."

The very next day strange events began to happen in the Donovan home that were initially interpreted as acts of vandalism. Ted Donovan's car had "sparkplug wires pulled out, rubber hoses unfastened, and the fan belt cut." Patty's car would not start and "mechanics surmised that internal engine parts had been disassembled." Car tires went flat—

apparently slashed with a knife. Other acts included: a door-bell "torn out of its housing," "shrubs were yanked out," and a "six-foot cast-iron pipe" on the roof was "bent at a ninety-degree angle." During this period, Patty could not contact "her invisible boyfriend on the Ouija board." Each time she tried, the planchette slid to GOOD BYE on the board. At this point, she did not connect the so-called vandalism with her request for the spirit's manifestation.

Finally, Ted Donovan contacted the police about the damage to their home and cars. During the second week of these strange events, while the Donovans were talking with their son Brian, "suddenly, all three heard something smash against a wall somewhere *inside* the house. . . they found a gaping eighteen-inch hole in the plasterboard wall in Brian's room." The same night they heard "scratchings inside the walls" of the house and "Ted also heard the sound of a board being pried loose." He investigated but found nothing. On the third week of March, the family heard strong pounding noises outside the house with no apparent explanation. Later in the week "sharp, jarring raps were heard inside the house as well," and these intensified. The scratchings and pound-ings continued after the family went to bed, and the "sound of boards being torn off the walls could be heard throughout the small ranch house." By the weekend "the pressure valves on the steam radiators somehow became unscrewed, spew-ing hot water all over the walls and carpets." Ted repaired them, only to have them fail again and again, and in frus-tration he turned off the basement heat. "Meanwhile, the pounding became more frequent and intense." He did all he could to locate the source of the noises and eventually hired a plumber and a heating repairman. They found the furnace and radiators to be in perfect working order. Replacement valves on the basement radiators were undone as quickly as the plumber finished the work. He finally left, telling Mrs. Donovan, "Lady, you got yourself a problem!" Patty's car was now locked in the garage, but her tires were slashed again and "the poundings on the house and walls grew louder and louder," and "pictures and decorations fell off the walls from the force of the impact."

On the evening of March 31, as the pounding sounds continued, the lights went on and off several times, "then the television set went dead. As it did, the Donovans watched as the heavy wooden bedroom dresser eerily began to levitate a few inches off the floor." It twisted violently and "perfume and cosmetic bottles fell over and dropped to the floor and broke." With the dresser resting on the floor, the drawers began to slam "in and out by themselves." Next a heavy chair lifted several feet off the floor, dumped the folded clothes on it, and then landed on top of them. Pictures lifted off the wall and floated around the room, the bed collapsed with Ted and his wife Ellen on it, and the levitated pictures fell to the floor. The same night various sounds and noises were heard: a mewing kitten that became a crying baby, scratching sounds, ripping and tearing noises, "the sound of planks being torn off the walls—it seemed as though the whole house was being dismantled."

The intensifying pounding on the roof and the outside walls of the house "transferred themselves to the inside walls. Over the course of an hour the poundings made their way up the hallway and ominously stopped." Then suddenly, "jarring raps sounded on Ted and Ellen's headboard; as though the headboard was being hit with a hammer." The sound of furniture falling over in the living room was heard—then Patty screamed from her bedroom, "Something was *in this room* with me!"

"On April Fool's Day, it rained rocks" on the Donovan's house for about an hour. Mrs. Donovan called the police who watched as stones fell from the sky. "Desperate, Ted asked the police what to do. 'Call a priest,' they suggested." After dark, "furniture and objects in the house began levitating in the air in full view of everyone. Some of the items dropped to the floor while others were slammed up against the walls." This continued throughout the night. In the morning, "with the house a shambles," Ted called the rectory of a local

Catholic church. That evening in the basement, Ted observed levitating furniture and cleaning supplies spilling on the floor. He heard shrieks and noises and found obscenities on his son's bedroom door.

As the nightmarish conditions continued, the Donovans could not sleep, so Ted decided to move his family to a motel. But this did not bring any relief, because the manifestations followed them to their motel room: "Lights switched themselves on and off. Pictures left the walls, and once more the pounding started up." After returning from breakfast the next day, they found their motel room in chaos. The next night the manifestations continued, and the family was forced to return home, only to find the interior of their house a total wreck:

> The mixture of smells was unbelievable. Rugs and beds were saturated with spilled food, cleaning fluids, liquor, shoe polish, cologne, and perfume. Towels were stuffed in the toilets. Furniture in every room was knocked over, some of it broken. Across the walls were scribbled truly demented blasphemies in blood-red ink, and obscene accusations against God and Christ.[55]

On April 9, stones once again fell on the roof and continued to fall all week long, beginning at dawn and stopping at dusk. "Their number and velocity varied." About half of the stones that eventually hit the ground disappeared. "Inside the house, the anti-religious activity had become as violent as the stones falling on the roof." The refrigerator moved away from the wall to the center of the kitchen, a large blacksmith's anvil from the garage was found in the freezer, and Ted's heavy toolbox was found in the attic. "Worst of all, there now seemed to be a physical presence in the house" and "the terror was enhanced by footsteps, the rustle of clothes, and heavy breathing. Once when Ellen Donovan quickly turned around, she saw a black form standing in the room behind her."

On Saturday, April 13, six weeks after the nightmare began, Ted called the Warrens. As the Warrens questioned the family, they discovered Patty's involvement with the Ouija board. "She denied [that] her spirit friend could have caused the gruesome activity in the house. He was 'kind and understanding,' *not* cruel and destructive."

The Warrens asked Father Jason to stay with the family because they had to leave for a previous commitment. When Father Jason arrived, he observed the "scratchings and poundings, and the levitation of small objects." As he went to bed he "listened to all the terrifying sounds the Donovans had been hearing over the last month." In the four days before the Warrens returned, the priest saw objects levitate and felt an evil presence. Father Jason left when the Warrens returned and spent the night on April 18. With the family in bed, "the phenomena rose in full strength, beginning with gruntings, and other bestial sounds, followed by the sort of piercing, bloodcurdling screams one associates with a horror movie." The Warrens heard a ripping and tearing sound that then changed to a sound like boards being torn from the walls. The pounding sounds heard before were "upgraded into what seemed like the blows of a gigantic fist pounding on the house" so that it shook with the impact. All of these combined and continued for about an hour. The family "claimed that some sort of ultra-black figure had manifested and begun to move in" their bedroom. Ed Warren challenged the spirit to reveal its identity, "In the name of Jesus Christ, *are* you a demonic spirit?", with the following results:

> The double bed with the three Donovans on it rose eerily into the air and remained suspended, some two feet off the floor. Suddenly the dresser careened across the room . . . it smashed into the wall, whereupon the double bed crashed to the floor.
>
>   . . . Brian was *levitating* some two feet above the bed! . . . The boy was propelled with tremendous force

against the far wall, five feet away. The boy then fell to the floor in a crumpled heap.[56]

The next day, April 19, the Warrens witnessed even more supernatural events.

Obscenities and blasphemies showed up on the ceiling of the parents' bedroom, written in indelible red ink. More astounding still, as everyone watched, the wallpaper began to peel off the walls, one sheet at a time, revealing foul language and blasphemies, again written in blood-red ink, on the wall underneath! Pictures not only moved on their own now, they began to smolder and break into flames. Doilies and towels and scarves would suddenly ignite, and then, flaming, hurl themselves at someone in the room.[57]

The madness continued into the weekend. On April 23, Ted moved his family to his parent's house nearby. But the demonic presence followed them once again. Some of the same manifestations occurred and by the third "night the whole house was resonating with merciless poundings. The next morning, bathroom faucets and plumbing fixtures were violently wrenched from the wall by some unimaginably strong force." Father Jason was also under assault in his rectory cell.

On April 25 the Warrens met with Father Jason who had a key to the Donovan's home. They decided to enter the house without the family present.

Upon unlocking the front door, Ed discovered the whole place had been systematically vandalized. Lamps, tables, chairs, books, pictures, clothing, and furniture were strewn around the living room. The smell, too, was utterly repulsive. Anything that was fluid had been dumped and left to decompose. Walking through the house, Ed found beds turned over, drawers pulled out, and linens scattered everywhere. Indeed, anything movable seemed to have been ripped, torn, or turned upside down. In the kitchen, the contents of the pantry and refrigerator had been dumped in a pile on the floor, with dinner plates and silverware heaped on top of that. Sheer insanity.

Heading back down the hallway, Ed suddenly realized something was awry. A moment later, the house began to violently rumble and shake, as if an earthquake had just struck. Fearing the house might actually collapse on top of him, Ed tried to get to the front door, but he couldn't move![58]

Ed emerged from the house with "two long, deep slashes forming the sign of the cross" on his left arm. It was obvious that he was the focus of this attack, but ultimately the Donovans were the target. The Donovans returned that afternoon and restored the house to some "semblance of order." The events of April 27 through May 2, could qualify as the worst nightmare one could imagine.

What occurred in the home of Ted and Ellen Donovan between March 3 and May 2, 1974, is classified as a true diabolical attack. The terrible assault that lasted for sixty consecutive days came to an abrupt halt with the exorcism conducted in the house on May 2, 1974.

The case, and all its particulars, is now a matter of record. In his own files, Ed Warren retains a statement by Ted Donovan's brother who himself was an involuntary witness to the phenomenon in the home.[59]

Philip Donovan, Ted's brother, stated: "[Neither] I, nor anyone else in my family, have ever before witnessed or actually experienced anything so weird and terrifying. . . . When and if a review is completed, I firmly believe that the ultimate conclusions will eventually suggest that unearthly powers or influences were at work."

*D*emonic attacks and possession have long been a topic of interest and investigation. Shortly after the Mount Rainier case, an editor of the Jesuit publication *America* reflected on the possible significance of such an event:

> But what can God's purpose possibly be in allowing a human being, made after His own image and likeness, to be subject to what seems a degrading, horrible and foul domination by an evil far beyond our power of imagining? . . . Because the horrible nature of evil *is* so far beyond our ken, there is always the danger that we will begin to ignore and then deny something with which we have had little contact. We need at times to be shocked awake to the realization that there *is* sin, and that there *are* diabolical powers who instigate sin.[60]

I want to stress that demonic attack and possession are rarely seen in such extreme forms as in the cases cited here. I would agree with Leighton Ford's conclusion, "Satan will take far more captives by quiet subversion than he will by frontal attack."[61]

Notes _____

1. William Blatty, letter to the author, Nov. 13, 1972.
2. Gerald Brittle, *The Demonologist* (1980; reprint, New York: St. Martin's, 1991), 108–9. Ed's statement that "four out of ten" cases they investigated were connected to the Ouija board (*The Demonologist*, 1980) was increased to "about seventy-five percent" in his interview with Stoker Hunt (*Ouija: The Most Dangerous Game*, 1985). In my interview with Warren on October 17, 1992, he stated that presently, "about seven out of ten of our cases are Ouija-board related."
3. Edward Glynn, "*The Exorcist*: Then and Now," *America* (Jan. 19, 1974): 26.
4. Ibid.; *Religious News Service*, Jan. 4, 1974, 10.
5. Glynn, "*The Exorcist*," 26.
6. Charles Chaplin, "*Exorcist* Author Remembers Mama," *Los Angeles Times Calendar*, Sept. 16, 1973, p. 24. William Blatty, letter to author, Nov. 25, 1973.

7. D. R. Linson, "Washington's Haunted Boy," *Fate* (Apr. 1951), reprinted in *Exorcism: Fact Not Fiction* (New York: New American Library, 1974), 13.

8. Thomas B. Allen, *Possession: The True Story of an Exorcism* (New York: Doubleday, 1993), 5.

9. Linson, "Haunted Boy," 13–14.

10. Allen, *Possessed*, 6–8.

11. Linson, "Haunted Boy," 14.

12. Ibid.

13. Bill Brinkley, "Priest Frees Mt. Rainier Boy Reported Held in Devil's Grip," *Washington Post*, Aug. 20, 1949, p. 9.

14. Linson, "Haunted Boy," 14–15.

15. Ibid., 15.

16. Ibid., 15–16.

17. Brinkley, "Priest," 9.

18. Chris Chase, "Everyone's Reading It, Billy's Filming It," *New York Times*, Aug. 27, 1972, p. D-9.

19. William Peter Blatty, *I'll Tell Them I Remember You* (New York: Norton, 1973), 117–18.

20. Ibid., 117.

21. Brinkley, "Priest," 1. Dr. H. A. Kelly, a professor of English at U.C.L.A. and author of *The Devil, Demonology and Witchcraft*, studied for thirteen years in the Jesuit order. He stated that in 1960 he interviewed the priest who had performed the exorcism in the 1949 case. Kelly concluded that the youth's problem was not possession, but illness. He also discounts the reality of demon possession as a misinterpretation of the Bible, and views exorcism as harmful. Contrary to other published accounts, he claimed that the case was not seriously investigated before exorcism began. However, Archbishop Philip Hannon, who held the Washington Chancery Office in 1949, and "who said he has seen the full confidential report on the original exorcism, said that psychiatrists had exhausted all efforts to help the boy and that hospital treatment had also failed when contact was made with the Washington Chancery" ("*Exorcist* a Travesty, Says Bishop," *Eternity* [Apr. 1974], 10). Kelly presents his account in a cassette tape: "Exorcism: The Devil, Demons and Possession," (Pittsburgh, Pa.: Thesis, 1974).

22. Blatty, *I'll Tell Them*, 118–19.

23. Brinkley, "Priest," 1.

24. Ibid.

25. Champlin, *"Exorcist* Author," 1, and other sources.

26. Brinkley, "Priest," 1. According to Blatty, "The story in the *Post* proved accurate, except where it implied that the boy knew Latin. It is true that he was able to parrot long phrases, and even sentences, in Latin just spoken by the exorcist as part of the ritual. . . . But the parroting is easily attributable to the heightened unconscious intellectual per-

formance . . . as a possible concomitant of certain forms of hysteria" (*William Peter Blatty on The Exorcist from Novel to Film* [New York: Bantam, 1974], 22–23).

27. Kenneth L. Woodward, "The Exorcism Frenzy," *Newsweek,* Feb. 11, 1974, 63.

28. Brinkley, "Priest," 1.

29. Woodward, "Exorcism Frenzy," 64.

30. Ibid. "The Reverend John Nicola was able to review the original documents of the case and found them signed by no less than forty-one witnesses" (D. Scott Rogo, *The Poltergeist Experience* [New York: Penguin, 1979], 213).

31. Brinkley, "Priest," 9.

32. Rex Reed, "Filming of *The Exorcist*—It was Hell," *Los Angeles Times Calendar,* Nov. 18, 1973, p. 28; *Los Angeles Times Calendar,* Sept. 16, 1973, p. 24.

33. "Casting Out the Devil," *America* (Sept. 3, 1949): 574.

34. Ray Loynd, "The Film's Impact," *Los Angeles Herald-Examiner,* Jan. 27, 1974, p. A-3.

35. Blatty, *I'll Tell Them,* 119.

36. Champlin, "*Exorcist* Author," 24. Another well-known case of possession is that of "Anna Ecklund," a forty-year-old woman who was taken to the convent of the Franciscan Sisters at Earling, Iowa. It was "probably the most detailed account of an exorcism case in twentieth-century America." It took place between September 1 and 23, 1928 (Carl Vogl, "Satan in Iowa," reprinted in *Exorcism Fact Not Fiction* [New York: New American Library, 1974], 212–45).

37. William Peter Blatty, *The Exorcist* (New York: Bantam, 1971), 41–42.

38. Ibid., 79.

39. Ibid., 88.

40. Ibid.

41. Ibid., 88–89.

42. Ibid., 89.

43. Ibid., 112.

44. Oesterreichs' book was reprinted in 1966 (New Hyde Park, N.Y.: University Books). Other helpful works include: Montague Summers, *The History of Witchcraft and Demonology* (London: Routledge and Kegan Paul, 1926), chapter 6; John L. Nevius, *Demon Possession* (Grand Rapids: Kregel, 1968), and Malachi Martin, *Hostage to the Devil* (New York: Bantam, 1976). There are a number of similar works available on possession for the interested reader.

45. Francoise Strachan, *Casting Out the Devils* (New York: Weiser, 1972), 33–34.

46. Ed and Lorraine Warren with Robert D. Chase, *Ghost Hunters* (New York: St. Martin's, 1989), 150. While I admire the Warren's obvious con-

cern, sacrificial service, and years of experience in investigation and countering of the occult, I do not always agree with their approach and interpretation. I have difficulty with their Catholic ritualism and sometimes their interpretation of events violates a more biblically based theology (Brittle, *Demonologist*, 177, 193, 221, et passim).

47. Brittle, *Demonologist*, ix–x.
48. Ibid., 109.
49. The following summary of this story comes from Brittle, *Demonologist*, 222–31, used by permission.
50. Ibid., 222–23.
51. Ibid., 224.
52. Ibid., 228.
53. The following story and summary come from Warren, *Ghost Hunters*, 51–71.
54. The following story and summary come from Brittle, *Demonologist*, 135–70, used by permission.
55. Ibid., 144.
56. Ibid., 157.
57. Ibid.
58. Ibid., 162.
59. Ibid., 169.
60. "Casting Out the Devil," *America* (Sept. 3, 1949): 575.
61. Leighton Ford, "God's Exorcist," *Decision* (May 1974): 12.

9

Jane Roberts, "Michael," and the Channeling Connection

In his book *A Crash Course on the New Age Movement* Elliot Miller accurately states that "a new wave of spiritism is sweeping America—the biggest since the initial outbreak of the phenomenon in the mid-nineteenth century."

This contemporary expression "of spiritism is called the 'channeling' movement. Channeling could be called 'Spiritism New Age Style.'"[1] One may visit almost any library and discover books about how to channel and the channeling movement, including *How to Develop Your ESP Power* (1966); *The Seth Material* (1970); *Seth Speaks* (1972); *Messages from Michael* (1979); *More Messages from Michael* (1986); *Michael's People* (1988); *Channeling: The Intuitive Connection* (1987); *Opening to Channel* (1987); *Channeling: How to Reach Out to Your Spirit Guides* (1988); *Spirit Communication* (1989); *How to Meet and Work with Spirit Guides* (1992); and Jon Klimo's informative, sympathetic analysis, *Channeling: Investigations on Receiving Information from Paranormal Sources* (1987).

157

Jon Klimo explains the popularity of channeling in the mid-1980s:

> Cases of channeling have become pervasive. An increasing number of people are now seeking and following the guidance provided through channeling. Accounts of the phenomena are sweeping the media. Dozens of new books said to be channeled are cropping up in bookstores. Millions of readers have been introduced to the phenomenon through actress Shirley MacLaine's recent best-selling books.[2]

Klimo provides the following definition for channeling:

> Channeling is the communication of information to or through a physically embodied human being from a source that is said to exist on some other level or dimension of reality than the physical as we know it, and that it is not from the normal mind (or self) of the channel.[3]

Elliot Miller believes that "most cases of channeling can be described in terms of voluntary possession."[4] In comparing the outburst of channeling activity in the nineteenth century with that of the present, psychotherapist and channeler Kathryn Ridall observes, "If today channeling seems focused on spirit guides and evolved spiritual teachers from other dimensions, the nineteenth-century mediums focused on channeling messages from the dead."[5]

Jane Roberts

When did the modern history of channeling begin? Did the Ouija board play any role in launching and popularizing channeling? In other words, is there a Ouija connection? Some writers believe that channeling began with the spiritualist revival of the nineteenth century, but others believe

Edgar Cayce is the father of modern channeling. Klimo argues for a different starting point:

> I have decided to begin the modern era of channeling with the American channel Jane Roberts and her source "Seth." It can be argued that the publication and widespread distribution of millions of copies of the assorted "Seth" books, beginning in the early 1970s, brought channeling to broader public attention than anything or anyone in this century until then except for Edgar Cayce. The many books about the Cayce material began to surface in the 1960s, although Cayce's work had ceased with his death in 1945. Roberts' channeling spanned from the 1960s until her death in 1984.[6]

The *New Age Almanac* claims that Jane Roberts's books "introduced a new generation to mediumship in a nonspiritualist context. *The Seth Material* is generally credited with launching the phenomenon of channeling, which has become one of the hallmarks of the New Age Movement."[7]

The article on "Channeling" in *Harper's Encyclopedia of Mystical and Paranormal Experience* agrees.

> In the wake of the decline of spiritualism, channeled works were produced, but channeling itself did not regain widespread attention in the West until the later 1960s and early 1970s, when Jane Roberts began publishing her Seth books. . . . Roberts inaugurated a resurgence of channeling of higher entities, rather than spirits of the dead.[8]

As we have shown, the Ouija board often functions as a doorway to the occult, and so it is not surprising that Jane Roberts's psychic experimentation began after her husband Rob suggested that she write a do-it-yourself book on ESP. Neither she nor Rob had ever had any telepathic experience or even seen a Ouija board. She followed her husband's suggestion and submitted a book outline to her publisher without any real hope that they would accept her proposal. Much to her surprise, the publisher was enthusiastic about her outline and requested several sample chapters. Jane and Rob started by purchasing a Ouija board and experimenting with it. The couple had little faith or interest in the board, and their first two attempts failed.

But the third time the Robertses tried the board, the pointer began to move, supposedly spelling out messages from "Frank Withers" (pseudonym). Both of them were surprised that the board worked. By the fourth session on December 8, 1963, the pointer moved so rapidly they found it difficult to keep their fingers on it. The answers grew longer and for the first time made complete sentences. The "Withers" character was superseded by "Seth." The next two sessions with "Seth" added a new element: Jane began to anticipate what the board would later spell out. At the next session, the fourth with "Seth," she began to hear the words in her head at an increasingly rapid rate—she received not only sentences, but whole paragraphs before they were spelled out on the board. By the next session on December 15, not only did Jane hear the words in her head, but she had an impulse to speak them. Suddenly, without any explanation as to how or why, she began to speak for "Seth." At this point she was freed from the board—she would go into a trance and "Seth" spoke through her.[9] Her gestures, facial expression, and voice changed when "Seth" "borrowed" them. The voice is described as deep and sometimes loud, and more masculine than feminine.[10] Jane also had several "out-of-body experiences"—through her "Seth" diagnosed illnesses, identified the contents of sealed envelopes, described buildings at a distance, gave life readings, and materialized apparitions in a well-lighted room.[11]

The Robertses progressed at an incredible speed—their adventure began on December 2, 1963, and by the end of January they had received some 230 pages of typewritten copy.[12] In her second book, *The Seth Material* (1970), Jane Roberts is pictured with fifty loose-leaf notebooks (five thousand pages) of "Seth" communications that she had accumulated by that time.[13] From 1970 until her death in 1984, Roberts's transcripts of her "Seth" sessions produced approximately a book each year. The "Seth" teachings completely reject biblical Christianity and substitute a complex philosophy of reincarnation and evolutionary development.[14]

When Roberts's 1966 book (*How to Develop Your ESP Power*) was republished in 1976 with the new title, *The Coming of Seth,* it detailed the primary role the Ouija board played in initiating the "Seth" contact. The initial publication of the book was fairly unsuccessful. In fact one publisher refused the manuscript specifically because of "Seth's" appearance— if "Seth" were deleted, he would have published the book.[15]

> There were few reviews for the book, but I was cautioned in some of them against leading my readers astray by encouraging experimentation with the "Ouija" board—which, some said, could lead to psychotic troubles at best, or possession by evil spirits at worst.[16]

Later in the introduction Roberts writes:

> We began with the "Ouija" board. It's the most preliminary method of activating the other portions of the psyche, a method that is considered quite unrespectable and disreputable by most parapsychologists. . . .
>
>   But this is not a book for scientists. It is a manual for ordinary people whose only access to a laboratory is their willingness to open the doors to the laboratory of the private mind.[17]

Roberts's use of the Ouija board for channeling served as a model for others. Sanaya Roman began to channel through her spirit guide "Orin" as a result of reading Roberts's books.

About that time Jane Roberts channeled several books by her guide, Seth, which I read and loved. Several friends and I began to get together to discuss the books, and got a Ouija board to connect with our guides. We got messages immediately, and asked for the highest guide we could get. We wanted a guide like Seth.

That was how I first met Orin in 1977. Orin came through the Ouija board, announcing that he was a master teacher and that we would be hearing more from him as I grew more able to receive him. . . . We continued to get guidance from Orin once a week, and much information from another guide, Dan, who came through more often. Many friends came over for these sessions and we took 200 pages of notes.[18]

Following a car accident later that year, Roman began channeling directly. In 1982 she met Duane Packer who had read some of Sanaya's "Orin" readings. In 1984 Roman and Packer joined forces and began channeling together. Their guides, "Orin" and "DaBen," suggested that they teach channeling, and so they did.[19] Roman and Packer write, "In the last several years, we and our guides, "Orin" and "DaBen," have taught several hundred people to channel and followed them in the development of their channeling."[20]

Dr. Kathryn Ridall acknowledges that the "Seth" material opened her mind to channeling: "I would say that my reading of the Seth books had made me receptive to the idea that I might benefit from teachers on other levels of existence and that channeled information could be valuable to me."[21] In her discussion of several channels, Ridall notes that all except one studied the "Seth" material to developing channeling.[22]

With the rise of "Seth's" popularity, combined with Roberts' reluctance to become a movement leader, others began organizing "Seth's" following. Two "Seth" books were published by other authors: *Conversations with Seth* by Susan

M. Watkins (1980) and _Create Your Own Reality_ by Nancy Ashley (1984).[23]

Tam Mossman, a trade book editor for Prentice-Hall, began editing the "Seth" material in 1968, "and for over fourteen years he served as editor for all of the Roberts' 'Seth' books while Jane was alive. In 1975 he began to channel his own entity, 'James.'"[24] As the demand for his evaluation of other channeled material increased, Mossman quit his job to edit his own quarterly channeling journal, _Metapsychology_ (subtitled _The Journal of Disincarnate Intelligence_). Other "Seth" centers, societies, and publications also emerged. After Jane Roberts's death, "other individuals appeared who claimed to be channeling Seth."[25]

Messages from Michael

All three "Michael" books prominently display Ouija boards on their covers. In his book _Channeling_ (published in 1987), Jon Klimo notes that "these books [_Messages from Michael_ and _More Messages from Michael_] have made 'Michael' one of the best known of the channeling cases that have come to prominence in the last few years."[26] "Michael" introduced himself through the Ouija board one evening in October 1970 to Jessica Lansing and her husband Walter (all names are fictitious) during a party in their home. Jessica and her husband were fascinated by parapsychology and the psychic. Craig and Emily Wright were present at the first session that lasted five hours.[27] This session led to the organization of the first Michael group, which continued to meet with "Michael" twice a month.[28]

Jessica later used a custom board because

> commercial boards don't hold up at all. I'd use one for a month, and then it would start to sag, or the letters would fade. We tried plastic coating them, mounting them on heavier backing, everything. They simply weren't designed for this kind of use.[29]

The members of the "Michael" group changed over the years, but Jessica continued to channel for the group for fifteen years before finally dropping out because of the demanding nature of the work. Other people served as channelers during the life of the group, including Camille Rowe, who used automatic writing instead of the board.[30]

The success of the "Michael" books and the related prominence of the Ouija board served to recommend the board as an initiation into channeling or as an occult tool. Indeed "Michael" himself endorses the Ouija board!

> Working with the board has the advantage that because of the speed at which the material is dictated, the medium is generally not able to interfere with what is being provided. This allows for more information and "monitoring," and has the advantage that when blocking of information occurs, the planchette tends to stop moving. . . .
>
> The speed is, of course, often difficult for those in attendance to follow, and while this is awkward, it also makes it possible for the ones taking the dictation to listen without jumping to conclusions, without attempting to guess the words.[31]

Chelsea Yarbro compiled *Messages from Michael* from ten years of transcripts of thousands of hours of Ouija messages. What do "Michael's" messages communicate about his worldview and his perspective on Christianity? The dust jacket of the book summarizes his views:

> Michael's messages are on the nature of the human soul and the purpose of life: belief is not required: you will reincarnate anyway. . . . There is no one "out there" when you exit who will ask you if you were an Episcopalian.
>
> In clear and beautiful language, Michael explained the seven ages of the soul as it reincarnates.

. . . Your soul type remains the same throughout its incarnations, though the soul ages as it matures. Finally the soul reaches the last threshold of death before life in another world. . . . Michael's messages fortify our hope that there is a meaning to life. . . . For once you pick up this book, as Michael said, you now have access to eternity.[32]

As you might anticipate, "Michael's" comments on theological matters are not compatible with the Bible. For example, he denies the existence of God, sin, evil, the Devil, and demons. While denying Christ's virgin birth and vicarious atonement, "Michael" asserts that Jesus was married and did not die on the cross. He also rejects the Resurrection because of his view on reincarnation.[33]

As in the case of "Seth," others claim to channel "Michael." Klimo writes, "Recently, more than half a dozen others in the San Francisco area have been claiming to channel the same 'Michael' by various means, including automatic writing, light trance, and full trance."[34] One such person is clinical psychologist and channeler Jose Stevens, who read some early messages of the original group.[35]

In answer to the question concerning the Ouija board's role in the launching and popularizing of the channeling movement, the evidence presented in this chapter shows that Jane Roberts's "Seth" material and the "Michael" books played a crucial and pivotal role in starting and spreading the channeling movement—New Age spiritism.[36]

Notes _____

1. Elliot Miller, *A Crash Course on the New Age Movement* (Grand Rapids: Baker, 1989), 141.
2. John Klimo, *Channeling: Investigations on Receiving Information from Paranormal Sources* (Los Angeles: Tarcher, 1987), 1. Permission to quote granted by Tarcher and Klimo.
3. Ibid., 2.
4. Miller, *Crash Course,* 142.

5. Kathryn Ridall, *Channeling: How to Reach Out to Your Spirit Guides* (New York: Bantam, 1988), 23.

6. Kilmo, *Channeling*, 23.

7. J. Gordon Melton, Jerome Clark, and Aidan A. Kelly, *New Age Almanac* (Chicago: Visible Ink Press, 1991), 96.

8. Rosemary E. Guiley, *Harper's Encyclopedia of Mystical and Paranormal Experience* (San Francisco: HarperCollins, 1991), 89.

9. Jane Roberts, *The Seth Material* (Englewood Cliffs, N.J.: Prentice-Hall, 1970), 13–21. The information on these sessions is not in exact agreement with that given in her first book, *How to Develop Your ESP Power* (New York: Frederick Fell, 1966), 16–17.

10. Ibid., 143–50.

11. Ibid., opposite inside cover of paperback edition, 72, 102, 106.

12. Ibid., 50.

13. Ibid., opposite, 177.

14. Roberts, *Seth Material*, 244–47; *The God of Jane* (Englewood Cliffs, N.J.: Prentice-Hall, 1981), chap. 20. For a summary on Jane Roberts and the "Seth" material see Stoker Hunt, *Ouija: The Most Dangerous Game* (New York: Barnes and Noble), 36–43.

15. Jane Roberts, *The Coming of Seth* (New York: Pocket Books, 1976), xi.

16. Ibid., xii.

17. Ibid., xv.

18. Sanaya Roman and Duane Packer, *Opening to Channel: How to Connect with Your Guide* (Tiburon, Calif.: Kramer, 1987), 127–28.

19. Ibid., 130–31, 135.

20. Ibid., 2.

21. Ridall, *Channeling*, 2.

22. Ibid., 33.

23. Melton, *New Age*, 97.

24. Klimo, *Channeling*, 135.

25. Melton, *New Age*, 97.

26. Klimo, *Channeling*, 50.

27. Chelsea Q. Yarbro, *Messages from Michael* (New York: Berkley, 1979), 17–28.

28. Chelsea Q. Yarbro, *Michael's People* (New York: Berkley, 1988), 2.

29. Yarbro, *Messages*, 49.

30. Yarbro, *More Messages from Michael* (New York: Berkley, 1986), 166–68.

31. Ibid., 167.

32. Yarbro, *Messages*, dust jacket.

33. Ibid., chaps. 9 and 10.

34. Klimo, *Channeling*, 50.

35. Ibid., 140.

36. Miller, *Crash Course*, 141.

10

The Biblical View of Demons, Demonic Activity, and Possession

Although the current tendency is to view all demonic phenomena as psychological,[1] the possibility of the demonic and of possession demand serious consideration. "The term 'possession' is misleading and is not the best translation for the Greek word *daimonidzomai,* which literally means 'to be demonized' and can often best be translated by 'to have a demon.'"[2] With this understanding, we will still use the word "possession," because it is commonly used by writers on this subject.

Without doubt, Jesus Christ taught the reality of demons and their activities. In fact Jesus claimed that his ability to drive out demons was a sign that the kingdom of God had come (Luke 11:20). Other biblical writers clearly distinguish between normal illness or disease and cases of demon possession (cf. Matt. 4:23–24; 8:16; 10:1; Mark 1:32; Luke 4:33–36, 40–41; 6:17–18; 9:1–2).

Missionaries have dealt with thousands of cases of demonic activity and possession. Dr. L. Nelson Bell, who was co-founder and executive editor of *Christianity Today*, writes: "I am ready to believe that demon possession is a reality in the twentieth century, for I have seen a number of cases in China. . . . Demon possession was as demonstrable an entity as malaria."[3] Prof. Raymond B. Buker, Sr., missionary to Burma for sixteen years and foreign missions secretary and professor of missions with the Conservative Baptists, agrees: "Those of us who have served on mission fields are aware of the reality of demonic activities. Many of us have seen demon-possessed people in action."[4] After discussing cases in Pakistan, China, Latin America, Africa, and America, Buker concludes, "We hold that demon possession is prevalent today even in the midst of our sophisticated society."[5]

The classic work on possession from a Christian perspective is Dr. John L. Nevius's *Demon Possession and Allied Themes*.[6] As a missionary in China, Dr. Nevius began to study possession, using a detailed questionnaire that he distributed to Chinese Christians and missionaries. Nevius concluded that demon possession was exactly what the name suggests.[7] In the preface to the reprint, Dr. Merrill F. Unger writes:

> One cannot peruse Dr. Nevius' account of his experiences with demonism as a Christian missionary in China, without being struck by the fact that it reads like a page from the Gospels where demon possession and expulsion play so large a part in the earthly ministry of our Lord.
>
> Today people in general, even Christians who profess to believe the Bible, dismiss the demonism of the Gospels and of the Scriptures as a whole, as an adaptation to the folklore and superstition of a bygone day, now no longer credible in a scientifically enlightened age.
>
> Dr. Nevius' firsthand contact with the rampant evil spiritual forces behind an ancient pagan culture not only proves that the demonism of the Bible is not

an adaptation to popular superstitions of the day, but is a spiritual reality of far-reaching import in our modern world.[8]

Unger's *Demons in the World Today* affirms the continuing existence of demons: "Evidence from Scripture, nature, history of comparative religions, and human experience all testify to the existence of evil supernaturalism."[9]

Millard J. Erickson, dean and professor of theology at Bethel Theological Seminary, notes:

> There is no reason to believe that demon possessions are restricted to the past. There are cases, especially but not exclusively in less developed cultures, which seem to be explainable only on this basis. The Christian should be alert to the possibility of demon possession occurring today. At the same time, one should not too quickly attribute aberrant physical and psychical phenomena to demon possession.[10]

Kurt Koch's *Occult Bondage and Deliverance* contains a significant discussion by Dr. Alfred Lechler, a German Christian psychiatrist. Lechler defines the demonic and distinguishes between disease and possession, examining diseases such as schizophrenia, epilepsy, mental depression, neuroses, psychopathy, and senile dementia.[11]

Lechler concludes: "Are we justified in talking about the demonic? Most definitely! People are today recognizing more and more that the demonic is by no means just some outdated biblical concept." To him the demonic is "a terrible reality with which one must ever increasingly reckon today."[12] In *Christian Counseling and Occultism*, Koch introduces and then quotes from Lechler's "Damonie und Seelenstorung."

> He presents three cases of possession and shows that they cannot be explained satisfactorily from the psychiatric standpoint. He concludes his differential di-

agnosis with the statement, "That in the consideration of this situation we were dealing with a possession was no longer doubtful to me. Since the condition would not improve despite thorough pastoral care, we proceeded to expulsion. This often resulted in violent struggles of some hours duration with flailing, screaming, mocking, cursing, especially when the blood of Christ was mentioned."[13]

In his lecture "Demonology Past and Present," Koch refers to a presentation he made to a group of London psychiatrists.

During the discussion which followed my talk, two psychiatrists stood up and stated quite dogmatically that possession as such did not exist. Immediately after this, however, two other psychiatrists present— they were both Christians—rose to their feet and said that they were not only convinced that possession was a genuine phenomenon, but that they had already come across cases of it within their own practice, one of them seven cases and the other eleven.[14]

Psychotherapist M. Scott Peck devotes a chapter of his *People of the Lie* to possession and exorcism. As one might expect, as a psychotherapist he did not believe in possession. "Of course I did not believe possession existed. In fifteen years of busy psychiatric practice I had never seen anything faintly resembling a case."[15] Peck admitted that his failure to observe a case did not altogether rule out possession, but he found the literature on the topic mostly naive, simplistic, or sensational. A few authors seemed more professional and viewed possession as rare. Peck decided to investigate and informed other professionals that he wanted to observe any supposed cases of possession. The first two cases he observed were afflicted with standard psychiatric disorders, but the third case actually was a case of possession. And later he was involved in a second case of genuine possession and was present at both exorcisms.

> As a hardheaded scientist . . . [I could] explain 95 percent of what went on in these two cases by traditional psychiatric dynamics. . . . But I am left with a critical 5 percent I cannot explain in such ways. I am left with the supernatural—or better yet, subnatural. I am left with what [Malachi] Martin [in _Hostage to the Devil_] called the Presence.[16]

Peck maintains that Martin's book "describes quite well five cases of possession," and that all of his (Peck's) "experience confirms the accuracy and depth of understanding of Martin's work."[17]

One case from _Hostage to the Devil_[18] concerns Carl, a psychologist and university professor involved in parapsychological research for a number of years. His experience eventually led to possession and the need for exorcism, followed by eleven months of hospitalization. Later he wrote a letter to his former students and colleagues, stating, "Solemnly and of my own free will, I wish to acknowledge that knowingly and freely I entered into possession by an evil spirit. And although that spirit came to me under the guise of saving me, perfecting me, helping me to help others, I knew all along it was evil."[19]

In the newspaper article, "Exorcisms Defended by Psychiatrist-author," Peck told the reviewer that since the publication of _People of the Lie,_ he knew of three other respected psychiatrists that were involved in exorcisms.

> [Peck] predicts that within a decade demonic possession will be a psychiatric diagnosis. He agrees with Malachi Martin, an expert on exorcisms, that 1,000 exorcisms a year are conducted in the United States . . . without the church's blessing.[20]

These respected and competent professionals attest to the reality of demonic activity and possession, and many others could be added if space permitted.

The Biblical Designation of Demons

Although there are about eighty references to demons in the New Testament,[21] they are only mentioned occasionally in the Old Testament (Lev. 17:7; Deut. 32:17; Ps. 106:37).[22] The King James Version (KJV) of the Bible does not contain the word *demon*, but usually uses the word *devil(s)*, a translation of the Greek words *daimon* or *daimonion* (Matt. 7:22; 8:31; Mark 1:34; 3:15; Luke 4:33, 35; 8:2; John 10:20; 1 Cor. 10:20), and other forms of the root word *daimon* (Matt. 8:16, 28, 33; 12:22; 15:22; Mark 5:16–18). On fewer occasions demons are referred to as *spirits*, and the qualifying adjectives or the context clarify that these are evil beings. The following references are taken from the New American Standard Bible (NASB).

1. "Spirits" (*pneumata*). "They brought to Him many who were demon-possessed; and He cast out the *spirits* with a word, and healed all who were ill" (Matt. 8:16).

2. "Unclean spirits" (*akatharton*). "He gave them authority over *unclean spirits*, to cast them out" (Matt. 10:1). *Akatharton* is translated as *foul spirit* twice in the KJV (Mark 9:25; Rev. 18:2).

3. "Evil spirits" (*poneron*). "He cured many people of diseases and afflictions and *evil spirits*" (Luke 7:21). Matthew 12:45 speaks of "seven other spirits *more wicked* [*ponerotera*, or "more evil"] than itself."

4. "Deaf (*alalon*) and dumb (*kophon*) spirit." "He rebuked the unclean spirit, saying to it, 'You *deaf and dumb spirit*, I command you, come out of him and do not enter him again'" (Mark 9:25).

5. "Spirit of infirmity" (*astheneias*). The KJV reads, "And, behold, there was a woman who had a *spirit of infirmity* eighteen years" (Luke 13:11). The NASB translates it, "And be-

172

hold, there was a woman who for eighteen years had had a *sickness caused by a spirit.*"

6. "Spirit of divination" (*puthona*). "A certain slave-girl having a *spirit of divination* met us, who was bringing her masters much profit by fortunetelling" (Acts 16:16).

7. "Deceitful spirits" (*planos*). "But the Spirit explicitly says that in later times some will fall away from the faith, paying attention to *deceitful spirits* and doctrines of demons" (1 Tim. 4:1). The KJV renders *planos* as "seducing."

The depravity of demons is amply demonstrated by their wicked characteristics ("unclean," "evil," etc.) and what they do to their victims (Luke 9:38–42). While all are depraved, some reveal a greater degree of wickedness ("more wicked" in Matt. 12:45).

The Personality of Demons

The Bible clearly teaches the existence of personal, invisible, spiritual beings called demons. Christians should have no difficulty in accepting the reality of the demonic if they accept the authority of Scripture. However, many contemporary theologians no longer adhere to an infallible and inerrant Bible, so it is not surprising that they dismiss the Bible's teaching on demons as the unenlightened thinking of Jesus' day when supposedly all emotional dysfunction was interpreted as demon possession. Others contend that Jesus simply accommodated his teachings to the people's superstitions, or that demons are merely a reflection of people's innate sinfulness. In *The Secular City,* Harvey Cox speculates that "the presence of repressed and projected feelings probably explains the demons of the New Testament period."[23]

If we accept the biblical account as both accurate and truthful, we must recognize demons as personal beings who possess intellect, emotion (sensibility), and will. Some theologians prefer to describe personality in terms of "self-consciousness, self-determination, and moral responsibility."[24] Since passages such as Mark 5:1–13 and James 2:19

demonstrate these attributes, we are justified in concluding that demons must have personalities. Unger points out: "That demons are individuals is attested by their intelligent and voluntary actions. They think, they speak, they act (Acts 19:15, 16) through a spiritistic medium or through a person over whom they have acquired control."[25]

The Origin and Identification of Demons

The Bible does not explicitly explain the nature or origin of demons, although various theories abound, including the following: (1) demons are an unenlightened explanation of disease; (2) demons are the spirits of disincarnate evil men; (3) demons are the disincarnate spirits of a pre-Adamic race; (4) demons are the disincarnate spirits of the "giants" (KJV) or "Nephilim" (NASB) of Genesis 6:4 (Unger views these as "incorrect theories" and "unscriptural identification"[26]); (5) demons are fallen angels, both confined and unconfined. This last explanation is accepted by most conservative Bible scholars as the one best supported by biblical teaching. Unger explains this position:

> In Satan's primal rebellion it seems that he drew with him a great multitude of lesser celestial beings (cf. Matt. 25:41; Rev. 12:4). . . . Those that are free are abroad in the heavenlies under their prince-leader Satan, who alone of the fallen spirits "is given particular mention in Scriptures." He is called "Beelzebub, prince of the demons" (Matt. 12:24), "Satan and his angels" (Matt. 25:41), and "the dragon . . . and his angels" (Rev. 12:7). These unconfined wicked spirits under Satan's kingdom and dominion, who are his emissaries and subjects (Matt. 12:26) and who are so numerous as to make their power practically ubiquitous, seem to be identical *with* demons. *If* Satan's angels and the demons are *not* identical, then no *other* origin of demons is anywhere explicitly revealed in Scripture.[27]

Some Bible scholars distinguish fallen angels from demons as still other created spirit creatures who followed Satan in rebellion.[28]

Demonic Activities

What does the Bible reveal concerning the activities of demons? Charles R. Smith's summary is helpful.

1. They sometimes promote idolatry (Acts 16:16; I Cor. 10:20; Rev. 9:20).
2. Since Satan is not omnipresent they are necessary to him to extend his power (Eph. 6:11, 12).
3. They can cause mental disorders (Lk. 9:39; Mk. 5:15).
4. They can inflict physical ailments (Mt. 9:32, 33).
5. They are sometimes responsible for the dissemination of false doctrine (I Tim. 4:1; I Kings 22:22; Rev. 16:13; I John 4:1–3).
6. They may be used of God to carry out His purposes (I Kings 22:22; II Cor. 12:7; I Sam. 16:14).
7. They sometimes seduce humans into immoral activities (I Tim. 4:1–3).
8. They have power to work "miracles" ("signs") to deceive men (Rev. 16:14; 13:12–15).
9. They sometimes attempt to instigate jealousy, faction, and pride among believers (James 3:13–16).
10. They may impart superhuman strength (Mk. 5:4).
11. They sometimes act as "fortune tellers" and prophets. The damsel who was possessed by a "spirit of Python" furnishes a New Testament example of this [Acts 16:16]. . . . Many of the "familiar spirits" of the Old Testament may have been such demons.
12. They exercise their power and influence in human governments (Eph. 6:12; Dan. 10:13).
13. They may enter and control human beings (Mt. 12:45).[29]

This last activity of entering and controlling people leads us to examine briefly demon possession in the Bible.

Demon Possession

Unger notes:

> Probably no phase of Biblical demonology has called forth more speculation, or excited more doubt and skepticism, than that dealing with the strange phenomenon of demon possession. Unbelief and rationalistic criticism have struggled desperately with this baffling theme, which is at once inexplicable and unmanageable to incredulity. The whole subject is at the same time rendered more acute because of the remarkable prominence accorded demon inhabitation in Scripture, especially during the life and ministry of our Lord.[30]

Most people's skepticism and reluctance to accept the reality of demons or demon possession is vividly illustrated by the character of Father Damien Karras in Blatty's *The Exorcist*. Although the girl Regan already manifested most symptoms of *extreme* possession, and Karras himself recognized *"the syndrome of demonic possession,"* he was able to rationalize the symptoms and conclude, *"'What's the answer, then? Genuine possession? A demon?' He looked down and shook his head. 'No way. No way.'"*[31] Karras's reluctance is typical of the general public's reaction to demon possession.

Unger's clear definition of demon possession is quoted here in full.

> Demon possession is a condition in which one or more evil spirits or demons inhabit the body of a human being and can take complete control of their victim at will. By temporarily blotting out his consciousness, they can speak and act through him as

their complete slave and tool. The inhabiting demon (or demons) comes and goes much like the proprietor of a house who may or may not be "at home." When the demon is "at home," he may precipitate an attack. In these attacks the victim passes from his normal state, in which he acts like other people, to the abnormal state of possession.

The condition of the afflicted person in the "possessed" state varies greatly. Sometimes it is marked by depression and deep melancholy, sometimes by vacancy and stupidity that resemble idiocy. Sometimes the victim may be ecstatic or extremely malevolent and wildly ferocious. During the transition from the normal to the abnormal state, the victim is frequently thrown into a violent paroxysm, often falling to the ground unconscious, foaming at the mouth with symptoms similar to epilepsy or hysteria.

The intervals between attacks vary greatly from an hour or less to months. Between attacks, the subject may be healthy and appear normal in every way. The abnormal or demonized stages can last a few minutes or several days. Sometimes the attacks are mild; sometimes they are violent. If they are frequent and violent, the health of the subject suffers.[32]

What are the symptoms of demon possession? The extreme case of the demonized man of Gadara (Gerasa) in the synoptics (Matt. 8:28–34; Mark 5:1–20; Luke 8:26–39)[33] clearly presents many aspects of the demonic invasion of the personality. This is the most spectacular case of possession in the Bible. The following passage is Mark 5:1–20:

And they came to the other side of the sea, into the country of the Gerasenes. And when He had come out of the boat, immediately a man from the tombs with an unclean spirit met Him, and he had his dwelling among the tombs. And no one was able to bind him anymore, even with a chain; because he had often been bound with shackles and chains, and the chains had been torn apart by him, and the shackles broken in pieces, and no one was strong enough to subdue him. And constantly night and day, among the tombs and in the mountains, he was crying out and gashing himself with stones. And seeing Jesus from a distance, he ran up and bowed down before Him; and crying out with a loud voice, he said, "What do I have to do with You, Jesus, Son of the Most High God? I implore You by God, do not torment me!" For He had been saying to him, "Come out of the man, you unclean spirit!" And He was asking him, "What is your name?" And he said to Him, "My name is Legion; for we are many." And he began to entreat Him earnestly not to send them out of the country.

Now there was a big herd of swine feeding there on the mountain. And the demons entreated Him, saying, "Send us into the swine so that we may enter them." And He gave them permission. And coming out, the unclean spirits entered the swine; and the herd rushed down the steep bank into the sea, about two thousand of them; and they were drowned in the sea. And those who tended them ran away and reported it in the city and out in the country. And the people came to see what it was that had happened. And they came to Jesus and observed the man who had been demon-possessed sitting down, clothed and in his right mind, the very man who had had the "legion"; and they became frightened. And those who had seen it described to them how it had happened to the demon-possessed man, and all about the swine. And they began to entreat Him to depart from their region. And as He was getting into the boat, the man who had been demon-possessed was entreating Him that he might accompany Him. And He did not let him, but He said to him, "Go home to your people and report to them what great things the Lord has done for you, and how He had mercy on you." And he went off and began to proclaim in Decapolis what great things Jesus had done for him; and everyone marveled.

This passage and the parallel accounts contain evidence of at least eleven characteristic symptoms of demon possession.[34]

1. *Incapacity to live normally.* Verses 2, 3, and 5 all refer to the man dwelling among the tombs. The area where this episode took place is burrowed with limestone caves and chambers for the dead—a place of isolation and death. Luke 8:27 states that the man "had not put on any clothing for a long time, and was not living in a house, but in the tombs."

2. *Indwelling by another being or beings.* Verse 2 notes that the man had "an unclean spirit." Luke says he was "possessed with demons" (8:27).

3. *Unusual strength.* Verses 3 and 4 indicate that the man was unusually strong; he could not be restrained even by "shackles and chains . . . the chains had been torn apart by him, and the shackles broken in pieces, and no one was strong enough to subdue him."

4. *Paroxysms.* It is obvious from the parallel accounts that the man experienced seizures of violence and rage. Mark denotes this by referring to the man's tearing apart the chains and breaking the shackles. Luke 8:29 says that the unclean spirit "had seized him many times," and Matthew 8:28 says he was "exceedingly violent."

5. *Inner anguish and self-destructive tendencies.* Verse 5 states that the man was "crying out and gashing himself with stones"—a reflection of his terrible inner pressures. Some cases of possession are accompanied by strong suicidal tendencies.

6. *Oppression and restless insomnia.* In verse 5 the man was active "constantly night and day," and Luke 8:29 says that he was "driven by the demon into the deserts."

7. *Visible conflict within the personality.* Psychiatrists would view this as a manifestation of a split personality or personality disintegration. This conflict appears in verses 6 and 7 when the man first "ran up and bowed down" ("worshipped" KJV) before Jesus, and then the demon manifested itself, crying out, "What do I have to do with You, Jesus. . ." This was a well-known Jewish expression meaning, "What do we have in common?"

8. *Reaction or opposition to Christ (or the things of Christ).* The demon's opposition to Christ is found both in the words quoted from verse 7 above, but also by the phrase "do not torment me!" Such resistance is a common characteristic of those who are demon possessed.

9. *Clairvoyant powers.* The demonized man identified Jesus without any previous introduction (v. 7). Demon possession may provide information beyond the knowledge of the person who is possessed.

10. *Speaking in different voices.* A characteristic common for demon possession—a voice change—occurs in verse 9. "And he said to Him, 'My name is Legion; for we are many.'" The name "Legion" should not be taken literally to refer to a Roman legion of six thousand, but to a large indefinite number of demons.[35]

11. *Occult transference.* In verse 13 the demons were transferred to pigs: "Coming out, the unclean spirits entered the swine." In transference the possessed person is delivered when the demons are transferred to another entity, in this case, the pigs. Kurt Koch notes that "transference never occurs in connection with the mentally ill, but only with the obsessed or possessed."[36]

What differentiates deliverance from demon possession and the cure of mental illness is the suddenness of the restoration. In this case, after the transference occurred, the man was well immediately—"sitting down" (in contrast to restless activity and paroxysms), "clothed" (instead of naked), and "in his right mind" (not demented). J. Stafford Wright's comments are pertinent:

The tendency today is to regard all the phenomena as of psychological origin. Yet Jesus believed in it [demon possession] and distinguished between normal illnesses to be cured by laying-on of hands or anointing, and demon possession to be cured by the word of command (e.g., Mt. 10:8; Mk. 6:13; Lk. 13:32). Any practicing psychologist who could cure "an extensive complex of compulsive phenomena"—as such possession has been called—by a word of command would soon be a rich man and would clear up the waiting lists that are a nightmare of psychiatry.[37]

Koch was a noted counselor and authority on the demonic with numerous direct experiences with possession. He developed four main criteria to identify possession.[38]

1. "The phenomenon of resistance." The possessed person builds up a resistance, anger, and violence toward the Christian praying in his presence. He may curse, blaspheme, and threaten to strike the counsellor. "He may even start to spit, tear a Bible up and throw it across the room."

2. "A possessed person can easily fall into a state of trance during a time of prayer." In this instance Satan attempts to cut off spiritual help from the person in need of deliverance. Pastor Ernest B. Rockstad related his experiences with possession during counselling. The person may become unconscious after Bible reading or during prayer, before actual counselling begins. Rockstad immediately calls for the demon to release his hold on the victim and then attempts expulsion.[39]

3. "Possessed people often exhibit clairvoyant abilities." Rockstad maintains that some possessed people he has encountered manifest clairvoyance, even revealing the secret sins of the counselor or the identity of telephone callers. After deliverance, these people no longer possessed this ability.[40]

4. "Finally, possessed people sometimes speak in a language or languages in a state of trance which they had no previous knowledge of." Koch believes that this is one of the

strongest arguments against the theory that possessed people are simply mentally ill.[41]

Despite contemporary unbelief, denial, and agnosticism, the existence of the demonic remains a reality. Possession is attested by the experiences of a number of psychiatrists, missionaries and other Christian workers, and competent students of demonology. Most importantly, Christ himself and the Bible teach the reality of demons and demonic possession. Certainly demonic possession does not account for the majority of modern cases of severely abnormal behavior or mental illness, but in the light of the previous testimony and biblical evidence, a diagnosis of possession cannot be immediately ruled out.

Notes _____

1. For a brief discussion of this position see Kent Philpott, *A Manual of Demonology and the Occult* (Grand Rapids: Zondervan, 1973), 18–19, and Kurt Koch's *Christian Counseling and Occultism* (Grand Rapids: Kregel, 1965), 183–85. T. K. Oesterreich's *Possession: Demonical and Other Among Primitive Races, in Antiquity, the Middle Ages, and Modern Times* (New Hyde Park, N.Y.: University Books, 1966) is a classic book on the subject of possession; to which he gives a psychological interpretation. Dr. Kurt Koch uses the Oesterreich material in support of his biblical thesis in *Christian Counseling and Occultism,* 208–17. See also: W. H. Trethowan, "Exorcism: A Psychiatric Viewpoint," *Journal of Medical Ethics* 2 (1976): 127–37; Graeme Taylor, "Demonical Possession and Psychoanalytic Theory," *British Journal of Medical Psychology* 51 (1978): 53–60.
2. Walter A. Elwell, ed., *Baker Encyclopedia of the Bible,* (Grand Rapids: Baker, 1988), 611.
3. L. Nelson Bell, "Demons," *Christianity Today* (Dec. 8, 1972): 26.
4. Ray B. Buker, Sr., "Are Demons Real Today?" *Christian Life* (Mar. 1968): 42.
5. Ibid., 43, 48, 52.
6. It was first published in 1894 and then republished in 1968 under the title *Demon Possession.*
7. John L. Nevius, *Demon Possession,* 8th ed. (Grand Rapids: Kregel, 1968), 242.
8. Ibid., v.

9. Merrill F. Unger, *Demons in the World Today* (Wheaton, Ill.: Tyndale, 1971), 7–13. See the complete arguments on these pages. See also Unger's *Biblical Demonology*, 9th ed. (Wheaton, Ill.: Scripture Press, 1952), 35–40.

10. Millard J. Erickson, *Christian Theology* (Grand Rapids: Baker, 1985), 450.

11. Kurt Koch, *Occult Bondage and Deliverance* (Grand Rapids: Kregel, 1970), 133–90.

12. Ibid., 134–35.

13. Koch, *Christian Counseling*, 278.

14. Kurt Koch, "Demonology Past and Present," Inaugural Lecture at The Swaziland Christian University of Theology, 6–7.

15. The following summary comes from M. Scott Peck, *People of the Lie* (New York: Simon and Schuster, 1983), 182–83.

16. Ibid., 195–196.

17. Ibid., 183–84.

18. Malachi Martin, *Hostage to the Devil* (New York: Bantam, 1976), 385–488.

19. Ibid., 485.

20. *Daily News* (Woodland Hills, Calif.), Dec. 14, 1985.

21. For complete treatments see Unger, *Biblical Demonology* and *Demons in the World Today;* and Walter A. Elwell, ed., *Topical Analysis of the Bible* (Grand Rapids: Baker, 1991), 287–94.

22. Louis Matthew Sweet, "Demon," *The International Standard Bible Encyclopedia*, 2 vols. (Grand Rapids: Eerdmans, 1939), 2:829. For a discussion of the meaning of "demon" in the Septuagint see Unger, *Biblical Demonology*, 58–61.

23. Quoted in Russell T. Hitt, "Demons Today," *Eternity* (May 1969): 10.

24. Charles R. Smith, "The New Testament Doctrine of Demons," *Grace Journal* (Spring 1969), 28.

25. Unger, *Demons*, 23.

26. Ibid., 13; Unger, *Biblical Demonology*, 41. For a good discussion of the rejected theories see both of these books. See also C. Fred Dickason, *Angels Elect and Evil* (Chicago: Moody, 1975), 155–60.

27. Unger, *Biblical Demonology*, 52. See pages 52–55 for more on this view.

28. Hobart E. Freeman, *Angels of Light?* (Plainfield, N.J.: Logos, 1969), 73. Hobart's position is answered by Smith, "New Testament Doctrine," 34–35.

29. Ibid., 36–37.

30. Unger, *Biblical Demonology*, 77.

31. William P. Blatty, *The Exorcist* (New York: Bantam, 1971), 263, 266.

32. Unger, *Demons*, 102.

33. For a discussion of the variations between the Matthew account and that of Mark and Luke, see Gleason L. Archer, *Encyclopedia of Bible Difficulties* (Grand Rapids: Zondervan, 1982), 324–25.

34. Kurt Koch discusses "Eight Marks of Demon Possession" in *Demonology Past and Present* (Grand Rapids: Kregel, 1973), 136–41.

> We have no guarantee that the relatively brief descriptions of demonically-caused symptomatology found in Scripture were meant to be considered normative examples of possession across time and cultures. All that the narrative accounts of demonization found in the Gospels and Acts claim is that they are accurate descriptions of demonization of that time, not normative descriptions of demonization that can be used for all succeeding generations. Hermeneutically, it is more correct to accept the biblical symptomatic descriptions as suggestive criteria for diagnosis than as normative criteria (Henry A. and Mary B. Virkler, "Demonic Involvement in Human Life and Illness," *Journal of Psychology and Theology* 5 [Spring 1977]: 100).

35. "Legion," *Baker Encyclopedia of the Bible*, 2 vols. (Grand Rapids: Baker, 1988), 2:1322–23.
36. Koch, *Occult Bondage*, 59.
37. J. Stafford Wright, *Christianity and the Occult* (Chicago: Moody, 1971), 129.
38. Koch, *Occult Bondage*, 64–65.
39. Ibid., 65. Ernest B. Rockstad, interview with the author, June 24, 1973.
40. Ibid., 66. Ernest B. Rockstad, interview with the author, June 24, 1973.
41. Koch, *Occult Bondage*, 66.

11

Conclusions

Is the Ouija board just a toy or game? For most of the general public, the Ouija is another amusement for children eight years and older, much like Monopoly® or Risk®. But our in-depth examination of the board has explored the Ouija's potential as a most dangerous game, especially for children and teenagers. Even people committed to spiritualism warn of the disastrous consequences that may befall the unsuspecting when they *play* with this formidable occult tool.

Why People Use the Ouija Board

If the Ouija board is not played merely as a toy, why do people use it? People work the board for a multitude of reasons: to contact dead friends or relatives, the living, or nonhuman intelligences; to develop psychic power; to find lost items; to predict future events; and to seek guidance.[1] These objectives are not amusement-oriented but strongly correlate with occult practices. In fact, it is the contention of this book that the Ouija board is an occult tool that may lead to entrapment and possession.

Our study of the history of certain occult devices—ancestors of the modern Ouija board—shows they were used for divination purposes, just as the modern board is today. People who naively approach the Ouija as a game are either ignorant or deceived about its possible consequences. Users who have dabbled with the Ouija board without obvious harmful effects either were never serious users or never had any results. Some participants believe the board provides them with useful information, perhaps about the future. Unfortunately, such communication usually includes a worldview that is diametrically opposed to Christianity. One such example is found in Stoker Hunt's interview with Ruth-Ann Campbell, who turned away from her Christian background and accepted spirit guides and reincarnation.[2] When Stoker Hunt asked Campbell's spirit guide Thomas, "What is the best way to prepare for death?" he was answered, "The best way to prepare for death is to study and accept the knowledge of reincarnation."[3] Other participants experience psychological trauma or the more serious manifestations of demonic presence and invasion.

The following additional sources also provide further proof that the Ouija board is an occult tool.

1. Occult skeptic Owen Rachleff concludes:

> Considered a game by many, the Ouija board is nevertheless a traditional object of veneration among occultists. Since the rise of spiritualism in the nineteenth century, this simplistic method of divination has gone through several cycles of popularity.[4]

2. Litany Burns, "a professional medium, clairvoyant and healer" and "an accredited teacher of psychic awareness in the New York State public school system," includes an entire chapter on the Ouija board in her book on developing psychic abilities. Her introduction states: "The *Ouija board* is not a toy; it is a *mediumistic* tool. *Ouija boards* have been used for centuries in Eastern cultures to communicate with *spirits* and to divine information."[5] Later she claims: "If you are just beginning to use your *mediumistic* ability, a *Ouija board* is a

good learning tool. It will enable you to gain a stronger sense of your own *mediumistic* process and the presence of your *spirit* and *guides*."⁶

3. In its court case with the IRS, the Baltimore Talking Board Company "made the contention that [the board] is a medium for communication between this world and the next and therefore does not in any sense constitute a game."⁷ Attorney Fisher argued, "We contend . . . that it is a form of amateur mediumship and not a game or sport. By means of this board one is enabled to get in touch with the other side."⁸

4. One of Parker Brothers' own brochures admits that the company does not know how the Ouija board should be viewed.

> Frankly, Parker Brothers does not know. *They are a leading manufacturer of games, but they doubt whether the OUIJA talking board should really be regarded as a game* [italics mine]. They *do* know that many people have a lot of fun with it, and that those who enjoy using it are often interested in the occult.⁹

A Biblical Perspective on Ouija and Other Occult Devices

Now that we have identified the Ouija as a device historically and currently connected with the occult, spiritualism, and divination, we will survey the biblical perspective on why it is wrong to use the board or similar occult devices.

1. The Old Testament contains numerous references to various kinds of divination and occult practices, all of which are condemned. The forbidden practices listed in the Old Testament are never described in great detail; apparently the Jews understood the various implications of the restrictions. No distinction was made between a "legitimate and illegitimate occultism. It was all under inflexible interdict, and traffic in it was, in all cases, viewed as flagrant apostasy from Jehovah and as a crime punishable by the severest penalties."¹⁰

Some of the major biblical passages quoted below make special reference to attempts by the living to contact the spirit realm, or in contemporary interpretation, other intelligences. The italics added below are mine.

Do not turn to *mediums* or *spiritists;* do not seek them out to be defiled by them, I am the Lord your God. (Lev. 19:31)

As for the person who turns to *mediums* and to *spiritists,* to play the harlot after them, I will also set My face against that person and will cut him off from among his people. (Lev. 20:6)

Now a man or a woman who is a *medium* or *spiritist* shall surely be put to death. They shall be stoned with stones, their bloodguiltiness is upon them. (Lev. 20:27)

And Saul had removed from the land those who were *mediums* and *spiritists.* (1 Sam. 28:3)

Then Saul said to his servants, "Seek for me a woman who is a *medium,* that I may go to her and inquire of her." And his servants said to him, "Behold, there is a woman who is a *medium* at Endor." (1 Sam 28:7)

The result of resorting to mediums and occult practices is reported in the following verses (italics mine).

So Saul died for his trespass which he committed against the Lord, because of the word of the Lord which he did not keep; and also because he asked counsel of a *medium,* making inquiry of it, and did not inquire of the Lord. Therefore He killed him. (1 Chron. 10:13–14)

And [Manasseh] . . . practiced witchcraft and used divination, and dealt with *mediums* and *spiritists.* He did much evil in the sight of the Lord provoking Him to anger. (2 Kings 21:6; parallel passage 2 Chron. 33:6)

Moreover, Josiah removed the *mediums* and the *spiritists* and the teraphim and the idols and all the abominations that were seen in the land. (2 Kings 23:24)

And when they say to you, "Consult the *mediums* and the *spiritists* who whisper and mutter," should not a people consult their God? Should they consult the dead on behalf of the living? To the law and to the testimony! (Isa. 8:19–20)

Deuteronomy 18:10–11 summarizes and condemns the offending practices of Israel's neighbors. (The key words are italicized for emphasis.)

There shall not be found among you anyone . . . who uses *divination*, one who practices *witchcraft*, or one who interprets *omens*, or a *sorcerer*, or one who *casts a spell*, or a *medium*, or a *spiritist*, or one who calls up the dead [*necromancer*—KJV]. For whoever does these things is detestable to the Lord; and because of these detestable things the Lord your God will drive them out before you. (Deut. 18:10–12)

The condemnation of "one who calls up the dead" ("one who consults the dead"—NIV) is all embracing, whatever the practice may be called. The terms in these passages and others dealing with the occult are frequently discussed by biblical scholars. The exact nature of some practices and the distinctions between them are not always clear. As J. Stafford Wright concludes, "Whatever may be the precise rendering of any single passage, it is beyond doubt that the Old Testament bans any attempt to contact the departed," as individuals or through a medium.[11] "This would obviously include attempts at do-it-yourself mediumship with a tumbler or Ouija board."[12]

What biblical reason lies behind the divine prohibition against these practices? In examining the passages that ban occult and spirit contact, authors Mark Albrecht and Brooks Alexander, provide two reasons:

> First: Such occult arts were held to embody negative spiritual energies. They were, in a word, spiritually "impure," and involvement with them was frequently compared to adultery. . . .
>
> Second: Participation in psychic or occult arts distracts us from faith in God and thus undermines the means of our salvation. It is a surrogate spirituality which panders to our lust for experiential gnosis (knowledge), reaffirming Satan's lie that our inherent spiritual resources are sufficient for salvation (i.e. we are God—Genesis 3:4–7).[13]

2. Nowhere does the New Testament indicate that the Old Testament prohibition on such practices was lifted.[14] When Paul and his companions were confronted by a "slave-girl having a spirit of divination" at Philippi, they did not view her ability with favor. Indeed Paul proceeded to exorcise the spirit, "'I command you in the name of Jesus Christ to come out of her!' And it came out at that very moment" (Acts 16:16–18). In Ephesus when God performed numerous miracles through Paul, including healing and exorcism, both Jews and Greeks came to Christ and openly burned their occult documents (Acts 19:11–19).[15]

3. Serious association with the occult can lead to apostasy—a departure from biblical Christianity. Rev. Stainton Moses and Edgar Cayce illustrate this principle. After reading numerous Ouija messages on spiritual matters, I am not surprised that people who believe them become apostates. These messages are correctly identified in Scripture as the "doctrines of demons" (1 Tim. 4:1). When messages from the Ouija board, automatic writing, and spirit contact are accepted as truth, they replace biblical authority.

4. From his vast counseling experience, Kurt Koch concludes that when a Christian becomes involved in occult practices "his spiritual life can be seriously affected. For the non-Christian there is often a real difficulty considering the claims of Christ and accepting Him as Savior."[16] In many cases participants strongly reject the gospel. John Kerr spoke with scores of people who were "deadly serious about framing a personal faith through the maze of the occult. They want a religious experience that the established faiths cannot, or will not, offer."[17]

5. Ouija board communications frequently turn out to be lies and deception. Actually, operators of the board can be deceived in at least three ways: (1) If the messages are only from the subconscious, the operator is deceived in thinking that they come from another source. (2) From a Christian perspective, if messages do not originate in the subconscious, their origin is demonic. (3) The message itself may be deceitful, designed to mislead the board user. English novelist G. K. Chesterton recalled how he played with the board as a youth. While he could not explain everything that took place, he was sure of one thing: "In the words that were written for us, there was nothing ostensibly degrading, but any amount that was deceiving. . . . The only thing I will say with complete confidence, about that mystic and invisible power, is that it tells lies."[18] According to Scripture, lying and deception are at the very heart of Satan's working in the world (John 8:44; 2 Cor. 11:13–15; 1 Tim. 4:1; Rev. 12:9).

6. Although the contemporary explanation for demonic activity and possession, both in the present and in the Bible, is psychological, the reality of the demonic demands serious consideration.[19] Dr. R. Kenneth McAll, a consultant psychiatrist, states that 4 percent of all his patients require exorcism and even suggests that patients should be asked if they have ever been involved in the occult. "This could range from playing with a Ouija board, following horoscopes, dabbling in spiritualism to practicing witchcraft."[20]

With the rise of occultism

> the conservative acceptance of both Satan and demons appears to be confirmed. . . . Spiritism has developed into a widely recognized "religious" practice whereby individuals seek contact with spiritual forces in an effort to gain aid or information for their own personal use. Such psychic phenomena as levitation, apports, telekinesis, automatic writing, and materializations are associated with spiritism. These activities appear to increase in intensity in proportion to an individual's openness to the spiritual influence. There seems to be a parallel between the characteristics of those who practice spiritism and those cited in Scripture as being "possessed."[21]

Jesus' ability to exercise authority over demons is an eschatological sign of the inbreaking of his kingdom (Matt. 12:24–29; Mark 3:23–27; Luke 11:18–20). Through the power of his word, Jesus cast out demons (Matt. 4:24; 8:16) or allowed them to depart (Matt. 8:32; cf. Mark 5:13). Christ gave this same authority to his twelve disciples (Mark 3:15; Luke 9:1), to the seventy-two (Luke 10:1–18), and later to all believers (Mark 16:17).

In our discussion of possession, we have noted that some cases require numerous sessions of exorcism over an extended period of time. In other cases, the demon comes out immediately. Some people are never troubled by any further symptoms while others seem to have periodic bouts with possession. What makes the difference?

Scripture provides several principles that determine how effective any particular exorcism may be. (1) The authority of the person (or preferably team) performing the exorcism must come from Christ. Jesus never had any trouble casting out demons, but his disciples did. In Mark 9 they were unable to cast out the demon from a young boy. When Jesus returns, the father asks him to heal the boy "if he can."

Jesus reminds the father that "all things are possible to him who believes" (v. 23) And the boy's father responds in faith: "I do believe; help my unbelief!" (v. 24). After Jesus successfully heals the boy, the disciples want to know why they were unable to cast out the demon. Jesus replies, "This kind cannot come out by anything but prayer" (v. 29—some manuscripts add "and fasting"). In the parallel account in Matthew 17, Jesus gives another reason why the disciples were unsuccessful in this case—they had so little faith. We may conclude that people involved in a deliverance ministry must be walking with the Lord, strengthened by his power, guided by his Spirit, and in an attitude of faith and prayer. (2) This account illustrates another point, namely that there are different "kinds" of spirits, some of whom are more difficult to get rid of than others. Some types of demons require special prayer (and perhaps fasting) on the part of the exorcist. (3) If the person with the demon does not truly repent and believe in Christ (as the father was requested to believe for his son in Mark 9) and renounce his or her involvement with the occult (or other sins as in Eph. 4:26–27), then freedom from possession may only be temporary. The demons can return, and the last state of the person may be far worse than the first:

> When the unclean spirit goes out of a man, it passes through waterless places seeking rest, and not finding any, it says, "I will return to my house from which I came." And when it comes, it finds it swept and put in order. Then it goes and takes along seven other spirits more evil than itself, and they go in and live there; and the last state of that man becomes worse than the first. (Luke 11:24–26)

7. What about the use of the Ouija board to develop the powers of ESP? This also can be a dangerous practice. "The deliberate cultivation of ESP . . . may easily bring one into the realm of the *occult*."[22] Jane Roberts began experimenting

with the Ouija board in connection with writing her book, *How to Develop Your ESP Power*. It wasn't long before she could communicate directly with her contact "Seth." Roberts's gestures, facial expressions, and voice changed as "Seth" spoke through her. It also is significant that material I received from Parker Brothers suggested that the reader obtain Roberts's book.[23]

When used with serious intent, the Ouija board represents a misleading path to spiritual truth. We have already amply illustrated its potential dangers to the user. Anyone not involved with devices like the Ouija board should definitely remain free of such devices for both their mental and spiritual well-being. The only supernatural experience God requires people to seek is him (Ps. 105:3, 4; Isa. 8:19, 20).

Breaking Free of Occult Practices

If you are currently entrapped in occult practices, it is in your own best interests to abandon your detrimental entanglement. How can this be accomplished? Although there is no universal pattern, here are some specific steps toward freedom:

1. Confess (or, for the Christian, affirm) your faith in Christ as Savior. This step is essential, for only the power of Christ is sufficient for full deliverance (Acts 4:12; 1 John 3:8; 4:4; 5:18). If you have been regularly involved in occult activity, your faith in Christ's ability to heal and cleanse you may be greatly diminished. You may need to seek out other Christians who will pray with and for you to be delivered.

2. Specifically confess each occult practice as a sin against God. Occult practices may have opened the door to other satanic inroads in your life, or certain sins may have led to your use of occult devices in the first place. Some sins that particularly and specifically need to be addressed may include: (1) anger and unforgiveness (Eph. 4:26–27); (2) lust, sexual immorality, or perversion (1 Cor. 5:5; 6:9–10); (3) hatred and violence (Luke 9:54–56; John 8:44); (4) envy, jealousy, and selfish ambition (James 3:16); (5) idolatry (1 Cor. 10:20;

Col. 3:5); and (6) blasphemy (1 Tim. 1:20). This confession may be done privately or in the presence of mature and understanding Christians who have some experience in dealing with the occult.[24] Extended Christian prayer support and competent Christian counseling also may be needed for certain spiritual and psychological dimensions.[25]

3. Renounce former activities and former associations (persons such as mediums), and dispose of occult materials and devices. At this point, reclaim any ground yielded to Satan and deny him any further ownership or right of influence. The principles of confession and renunciation are illustrated by the experience at Ephesus recorded in Acts 19:18–19.

4. Persist in your Christian walk. To experience the full victory of redemption through Christ, a person must heed the biblical instructions to "put on the whole armor of God" and "resist the devil" (Eph. 6:11; James 4:7). Become a part of a local church where the Bible is clearly preached and taught and join a small group study where you can regularly fellowship with other believers and be part of a prayer circle.

Notes

1. Stoker Hunt, *Ouija: The Most Dangerous Game* (New York: Barnes and Noble, 1985), 9.
2. Ibid., 51–53.
3. Ibid., 60. Other illustrations of such non-Christian beliefs occur in Jane Roberts's Seth material, the Michael messages, Ruth Montgomery's writings, and the conclusions of Gina Covina in *The Ouija Book*.
4. Owen S. Rachleff, *The Occult Conceit* (Chicago: Cowles, 1971), 196.
5. Litany Burnes, *Develop Your Psychic Abilities* (New York: Pocket Books, 1985), 185.
6. Ibid., 193.
7. *Baltimore Sun*, Mar. 4, 1921, evening edition.
8. *Baltimore Sun*, Feb. 10, 1922, evening edition.
9. *The Weird and Wonderful OUIJA Talking Board Set* (Salem, Mass.: Parker Brothers, n.d.) brochure.
10. Merrill F. Unger, *Biblical Demonology* (Wheaton, Ill.: Scripture Press, 1952), 144. See Unger for a discussion of demonology, divination, and necromancy.

11. J. Stafford Wright, *Christianity and the Occult* (Chicago: Moody, 1971), 112.
12. Ibid., 114.
13. Mark Albrecht and Brooks Alexander, "Biblical Discernment and Psychology," *SCP Journal* 4 (Winter 1980–81): 19.
14. Wright, *Christianity,* 112; Os Guinness, *Encircling Eyes* (Downers Grove, Ill.: InterVarsity, 1974), 47–48.
15. See the discussion of "Magic," in the New Testament in *The New International Dictionary of New Testament Theology* (Grand Rapids: Zondervan, 1976), 2:552–62.
16. Kurt Koch, *Between Christ and Satan* (Grand Rapids: Kregel, 1968), 124; *Occult Bondage and Deliverance* (Grand Rapids: Kregel, 1970), 33–35.
17. John S. Kerr, *The Mystery and Magic of the Occult* (Philadelphia: Fortress, 1971), 11.
18. Gilbert K. Chesterton, *The Autobiography of G. K. Chesterton* (New York: Sheed and Ward, 1936), 77.
19. See Unger, *Biblical Demonology.*
20. R. Kenneth McAll, "The Ministry of Deliverance," *The Expository Times* (July 1975): 296.
21. S. E. McClelland, "Demons, Demon Possession," in *Evangelical Dictionary of Theology,* ed. Walter A. Elwell (Grand Rapids: Baker, 1984), 307.
22. J. Stafford Wright, "Sorting Out the Supernatural," *His* (Mar. 1975): 4.
23. *The Weird and Wonderful OUIJA Talking Board Set.*
24. Jack Deere, "Demonic Inroads," from *Healing 92 Workshop,* VMI Inc.
25. For those who need additional information or counseling, I recommend *The 1993 Directory of Cult Research Organizations,* available from American Religions Center, P.O. Box 168, Trenton, MI 48183 (phone: 313-425-7788). The directory is updated periodically and lists organizations in the United States and abroad. About one hundred evangelical ministries indicate the occult as a focus, and about half of these provide counseling. Several of these ministries which deal with the occult are presented here:

> Answers in Action
> Robert and Gretchen Passantino
> P.O. Box 2067
> Costa Mesa, CA 92628
> (714) 646-9042
>
> Christian Apologetics: Research & Information Service (CARIS)
> Jim Valentine, director; Jack Roper, researcher
> P.O. Box 1659
> Milwaukee, WI 53201
> (414) 771-7379

Christian Research Institute (CRI)
P.O. Box 500
San Juan Capistrano, CA 92623
(714) 855-4428

De Gloria Outreach
Tom Poulson, general secretary
7 London Road
Bromley, Kent BR1 1BY
United Kingdom
(01) 464-9500

Occult Research & Crime Consultants (ORCC)
Greg Reid
P.O. Box 370006
El Paso, TX 79936
(915) 595-3569

Spiritual Counterfeits Project (SCP)
P.O. Box 4308
Berkeley, CA 94704
(510) 540-0300

Selected Materials for Further Reading

Albrecht, Mark. *Reincarnation: A Christian Critique of a New Age Doctrine.* Downers Grove, Ill.: InterVarsity, 1982. (Original title: *Reincarnation: A Christian Appraisal*)

Anderson, Peter. *Satan's Snare: The Influence of the Occult.* Welwyn, England: Evangelical Press, 1988.

Ankerberg, John and John Weldon. *Facts on Spirit Guides.* Eugene, Ore.: Harvest House, 1988.

Arnold, Clinton E. *Powers of Darkness: Principalities and Powers in Paul's Letters.* Downers Grove, Ill.: InterVarsity, 1992.

Crouse, Bill. *A Primer on Occult Philosophy.* Dallas: Probe, 1983.

Doorways to Danger. London: Evangelical Alliance, 1987.

Ernest, Victor H. *I Talked with Spirits.* Wheaton, Ill.: Tyndale, 1970.

"Expanding Horizons: Psychical Research and Parapsychology," *SCP Journal* 4 (Winter 1980–81).

Gudel, Joseph P., Robert M. Bowman, Jr., and Dan R. Schlesinger, "Reincarnation—Did the Church Suppress It?" *Christian Research Journal* 10 (Summer 1987): 8–12.

Guiness, Os. *Encircling Eyes: The Current Resurgence of the Oc-*

cult. Downers Grove, Ill.: InterVarsity, 1974.

Gruss, Edmond C. *The Ouija Board: Doorway to the Occult*. Chicago: Moody, 1975.

Hunt, Dave. *The Cult Explosion*. Irvine, Calif.: Harvest House, 1980.

Ice, Thomas, and Robert Dean, Jr., *A Holy Rebellion*. Eugene, Ore.: Harvest House, 1990.

Koch, Kurt. *Demonology Past and Present*. Grand Rapids: Kregel, 1973.

———. *Occult Bondage and Deliverance*. Grand Rapids: Kregel, 1979.

McDowell, Josh, and Don Stewart. *The Occult: The Authority of the Believer over the Powers of Darkness*. San Bernardino, Calif.: Here's Life, 1992.

Miller, Elliot. *A Crash Course on the New Age Movement*. Grand Rapids: Baker, 1989. Chapters 8 and 9: "Channeling: Spiritistic Revelations for the New Age." Also published in *Christian Research Journal* 10 (Fall 1987): 8–15; 10 (Winter/Spring 1988): 16–22.

Montgomery, John W., ed. *Demon Possession*. Minneapolis: Bethany, 1976.

Parker, Russ. *Battling the Occult*. Downers Grove, Ill.: InterVarsity, 1990.

Rawlings, Maurice. *Life Wish—Reincarnation: Reality or Hoax?* Nashville: Nelson, 1981.

Sall, Millard J. "Demon Possession or Psychopathology?: A Clinical Differentiation." *Journal of Psychology and Theology* 4 (Fall 1976): 286–90.

Unger, Merrill F. *Biblical Demonology*. Wheaton, Ill.: Scripture Press, 1952.

Virkler, Henry A., and Mary B. Virkler. "Demonic Involvement in Human Life and Illness," *Journal of Psychology and Theology* 5 (Spring 1977): 95–102.

Weldon, John. "Dowsing Gift, Human Ability, or Occult Power? *Christian Research Journal* 14 (Spring 1992): 8–13, 34.

Weldon, John, and Clifford Wilson. *Occult Shock and Psychic Forces*. San Diego: Master Books, 1980.

Index